ADVANCE PRAISE

"In the Vietnam War, the accepted rule of thumb was for every soldier out on patrol, nine other soldiers were in the rear to support him. In *No Wooden Nickels*, Don Boyce brings alive what it was like to be one of those nine. Serving as a First Lieutenant in the Medical Service Corps of the 91st Evac Hospital in Chu Lai, Vietnam, on the shores of Chu Lai Bay, Boyce shares the story of his year of duty, when on one day you might be called up to rescue a team of medical personnel who had wandered too far afield, and on another training to be a lifeguard in the choppy waters of Chi Lai Bay. *No Wooden Nickles*, part M.A.S.H. and part CHINA BEACH, is a walk back to a time long forgotten, to a land where America fought an unwinnable war."

— Susan Byrum Rountree,
Author of *Nags Headers* and *In Mother's Words*

"In his new book, *No Wooden Nickels*, Vietnam vet, Don Boyce shares his recollections of time spent in the war zone during 1970-71. Unlike many veterans who experienced direct combat serving in infantry or artillery units, Don spent his year in the Medical Service Corps. His assignment was the 91st Evac Hospital in Chu Lai, located in I Corp in the northern section of South Vietnam. He shares memories, anecdotes and personal thoughts of interest to veterans and non-vets as well. A good read indeed."

— Lou Eisenbrandt,
Author of *Vietnam Nurse* and *Unsteady as She Goes*

No Wooden Nickels

No Wooden Nickels

A REMF MSC's Tour at 91st Evac Hosp in Chu Lai

C. O. L. Boyce

Deeds Publishing | Athens

Published by Deeds Publishing in Athens, GA
www.deedspublishing.com

Printed in The United States of America

Cover design by Mark Babcock.

ISBN 978-1-950794-90-4

Books are available in quantity for promotional or premium use. For information, email info@deedspublishing.com.

First Edition, 2022

10 9 8 7 6 5 4 3 2 1

For my family who have made me what I have become, and to the men and women of the 91st Evac Hospital in Chu Lai

Contents

HOW TO READ THIS BOOK:

If you don't know what a REMF is, make sure to read the Forward. Chapters 2 through 7 are written as a continuum of how I wound up at the 91st Evac Hospital in Chu Lai and make more sense to be read as a unit. Similarly, the last two chapters go together. The rest can be read individually according to the reader's interest.

Foreword

I don't know why, but I always had an interest in returning to Chu Lai. Other vets, like my former boss, a tank commander in the Mekong Delta, and my brother-in-law, an ordinance specialist in Long Binh, had no interest whatsoever. Both were glad to be done with it when they returned to the States. Many reasons exist to explain their and other vets' feelings:

- They had such a traumatic experience that a revisit would revive too many bad memories?
- Possibly, they haven't come to terms with over 55,000 Americans dying for a lost cause?
- US public opinion in the post-Vietnam War years acknowledged we supported a morally corrupt side in the conflict in our war to prevent the spread of communism in South East Asia?
- Their memories still hold the video clips of our ignominious retreat from Vietnam in 1975 of helicopters evacuating the last Americans and a few Vietnamese from the rooftop of the CIA office building[1] in Saigon.

For me, I had, overall, positive memories of my tour of duty. Yes, there were hardships, but I liked the US and local people I worked with at the 91st Evac and could see the beauty in our surroundings, despite the wartime environment. Possibly, I just wanted to see if the hotels we imagined would spring up along the beach after the war had materialized in the peacetime that ensued since the 1980's. The beaches and bay at Chu Lai had all the hallmarks of being another Waikiki.

Not every soldier who's assigned to a combat zone is out on patrol, in fire fights, or encountering boobytraps, what we now call IEDs (Improvised Explosive Device). In the Vietnam War, the accepted rule of thumb was that for every soldier out on patrol, nine other soldiers were in the rear to support him. Wars are logistical operations as much as tactical fighting. During these times of Covid-19 pandemic, Americans have gotten an appreciation for logistics, or what we call the Supply Chain.

The support of a fighting force on the front lines includes supplies of ammo and food, equipment repair facilities, transportation units, and medical units. The units carrying out such support are usually located "in the rear," far behind the areas where active combat takes place. In WWII, the rear was a good distance from the "front lines" where the action was. All the territory behind those lines were won and controlled by the Allies' forces.

In Vietnam, we did not take and hold onto territory. We fought a different war, a guerrilla war, where no "front lines" existed and there was no easy way to visibly distinguish between a friendly and enemy citizen. We did have secure areas of sorts: Base Camps like Long Binh, Cam Ranh Bay, and Chu Lai and Fire Bases (FBs) and Landing Zones (LZs) operated by Army Divisions with responsibility for supporting combat operations in an assigned region. We'd take an area, killing as many of the enemy as possible, and then go back to our secure areas. Only to have the enemy, the Viet Cong (VCs) and invading North Vietnam Army (NVA) retake it later.

Base Camps were relatively large areas of several square miles to house all the facilities for support units to operations. FBs and LZs were much smaller but were defendable positions containing artillery support, along with limited mess and sleeping quarters for the soldiers who would go out on patrol. These FBs are what Oliver Stone depicted in his film, "*Platoon.*"

REMF is a derogatory term for the support personnel who operate in the rear: "Rear Echelon Mother F*r." In the Gulf and Afghanistan Wars they are called FOBbits for the denizens of Forward Operating Bases (FOBs). Baghram Air Base in Afghanistan is described as an FOB in Benjamin Tupper's book, *Greetings from Afghanistan, Send More Ammo* (p.110). It would be equivalent to a Base Camp in Vietnam.

The day-to-day life of a REMF is less risky than the combat soldier, but it's not without some difficulties. Probably the most difficult element would be overcoming boredom and homesickness which occupies your mind more than the combat soldier who's focusing on destroying the enemy while not being destroyed himself. The main risks to life for a REMF were incoming rocket and/or mortar attacks and accidental/non-combat death.

Time never moved so slow in the rear. When arriving in-country many of us said to ourselves, "364 more to go." We had "short-timer" calendars in our work or bunk space, often in the image of Charles Schultz' Snoopy. The Snoopy cartoon was divided into boxes numbered 1 to 364 for the days you had left in Vietnam. Every morning you'd fill in a square. These showed us how many days we had before we could "sky home" on an airplane.

I likened my experience as a REMF as going to a low-security prison for a year. Barring an unfortunate event, e.g., a rocket attack, or a jeep accident, you were highly likely to go home in one piece. You just had to do your time. Arthur Koestler's *Darkness at Noon* and Bernard Malamud's *The Fixer*, which I read during my tour, resonated with me. Both deal with protagonists unjustly imprisoned.

The remembrances on the following pages are those of an 1LT MSC (First Lieutenant, Medical Service Corps[2]) who served in Vietnam from July 1970 to June 1971[3,4]. You won't read of the life of a grunt as in James P. Brinker's *West of Hue, Down the Yellow Brick Road.* Rather, I hope it gives the reader a picture, with some humor, of what life was like in an Evacuation Hospital in Chu Lai in support of the American Division, a.k.a. 23rd Infantry Division. I acknowledge that I'm recalling these memories after having left Vietnam 50 years ago. While I've forgotten people's names, their faces are always with me. As imperfect as this may be, my intention is to report the ups and downs of life as an MSC REMF.

NOTES:

1. Newsreels usually identify the helicopter taking off from the rooftop of the US Embassy in Saigon; but, in fact, it was the roof top of the office building the CIA used during the war.

2. If the doctors (Army Medical Corps), nurses (Army Nursing Corps), Medivac pilots, and hospital corpsmen are the primary support to combat troops, MSCs are the support to the support, of lower standing, in my mind.

3. At that time, General Creighton Abrams led all operations in country after assuming command from General William Westmoreland. His policy of pacification operations, small regular patrols in a region, had begun to register promise in that Army Intelligence aerial photos showed more farmed land

spreading out from the main North-South route, Route 1, in country during my tour, July 1970-June 1971.

4. For a better appreciation for how General Abrams prosecuted the war from June 1968 to its end, read Lewis Sorley's book, *A Better War – The Unexamined Victories and Final Tragedy of America's Last Years in Vietnam*, Harvest-Harcourt, New York, (1999) 507 pages. Most histories of the Vietnam War cover the run up to the war and up to the Tet Offensive in 1968, which is a very incomplete picture! Abrams' small unit tactics was securing areas to allow farming to resume. The incursions into Cambodia in 1970 and into Laos in 1971 crippled the enemy's supply lines. Had Washington's politicians not tied Abrams' hands, an US invasion of North Vietnam in 1971-1972 probably would have been militarily successful.

1. Medcap Gone Wrong

COL Kenwyn Nelson was a tall man, probably around 6'4", with a head of bright red hair. Our third CO, he had transferred in from the 71st Evac in Pleiku, when it was deactivated. His nickname was "The Big Red One," keying off the same moniker for the 1st Infantry Division, whose shoulder patch is a big, red, numeral one on a field of OD green. COL Nelson, a thoracic surgeon, seemed to value his MSC officers as he treated us as equals in the unit, whereas our second XO, an MSC LTC, did not.

I was puttering around the motor pool mid-afternoon on an early spring day, probably about the time the Beatles had called it quits. That news left me feeling a loss I hadn't expected, as did the news that Jimi Hendrix and Janis Joplin had died of drug overdoses. A "Piece of My Heart" died when these two talents left this world too soon.

"Lieutenant Boyce, GET in here, NOW!" It was COL Nelson, yelling my name out the orderly room window. Anyone can imagine my distress; I ran to the orderly room and to his office to find out why a normally mellow guy wasn't.

He hit me with, "LT Boyce, our group of doctors and nurses that went to visit the provincial hospital in Quang Ngai this morning had a flat tire while out on a local road visiting a temple of some sort. They discovered there was no jack in the truck for them to change the tire. Why wasn't there a jack in the truck like there should be? I want you to get down there with a jack and get that tire changed so they can get back here before dark."

"Yes, Sir," I replied. Then I asked, "Where are they exactly?"

He didn't know precisely, only that they had left the provincial hospital to visit a temple. The only directions he had was, "…take a left at the road just before the bridge that goes into Quang Ngai."

Before about facing to leave his office, he added, "If anything happens to those people, I'm holding you responsible." My silent reaction, "GULP!"

I went back to the motor pool and told Woody, my motor sergeant, our situation. "Woody, we got an emergency. The docs and nurses got a flat tire sightseeing after their visit to the Quang Ngai Provincial Hospital. We need to take a truck with a jack."

"LT, they took my truck for that Medcap. When it left this morning, it had a jack in it." Woody piped up. "The only truck we have available is our 2-1/2-ton tow truck. I'll check to make sure it has a jack in it. So where are they?" he asked.

I could only repeat the scant information COL Nelson had given me. So, we headed out the main gate and turned south on Route 1 toward Quang Ngai. While I had never been outside the Chu Lai base camp, Woody had been "to the ville" nearby once or twice, but not much further than that.

Adding pressure to this situation was that Quang Ngai province is where Ho Chi Minh got up the Viet Minh to overthrow the French. So, this area was home turf for the Viet Cong. More importantly, I was nervous for the security situation and for not knowing where we were going exactly. We had no maps to take with us (and certainly no GPS back in those days)!

Outside the Chu Lai gate, Vietnamese men and women sat at make-shift tables along the road selling stuff, sort of a one-dimensional Arabian bazaar. There were tables with rose-colored gold jewelry, and I wondered if it was real gold, a gold and copper alloy, or some other metal altogether. We also passed mama-sans with large reed trays separating rice from the husks. They'd flip the lightly ground mix into the air and let the breeze blow the chaff away and catch the falling, denser rice with the tray.

In about 20 to 30 minutes, we got to the bridge into Quang Ngai. The only "road" to the left resembled a wide path and less of a road for motorized vehicles. Pedestrians were walking both ways on this unpaved lane. How to ask for directions since we didn't speak Vietnamese? We didn't even have a map to help get directions with crude sign language. I knew the symbol for temple in Buddhism looked like a swastika; so, I drew it in the dust on our tailgate. I pointed to it and tried to query a passing man who blew me off as if I didn't exist. I thought I saw a knowing look from a woman who went by; so, Woody and I decided to take a chance with the lane. It would be dark soon and we needed to get the crew back before nightfall.

Our guess turned out to be the right one. We spotted the truck not too far down the road in an open area. The docs, nurses, and 1LT John Messina were out of the vehicle amid a bunch of local people. "Boyce, am I glad to see you!" exclaimed Messina, relief evident in his voice. "I've been trying to get our folks to shoo the locals away, but they want to visit with them." The locals that surrounded them had two motivations. One was looking for medical help for themselves or a sick child. Secondly, one of the nurses in the group was a blond, a curiosity to the Vietnamese women.

"John, we're just as happy to see you!" I explained the less-than-specific location directions we'd been given and our uncertainty in taking the road we did at the bridge. John was the only group member with an M-16. Woody had one and I had a .45-cal pistol, not that much firepower, or experience, to fend off an attack should there be one.

We got the tire changed quickly enough; loaded everyone up; and were on our way out of there. I was happy that we had found our group and got the tire changed. My lingering concern was getting back to Chu Lai before dark. As we started back in a two-truck convoy, the Animals *We Gotta Get Out of This Place* played in my mind.

We arrived back to Chu Lai with about a half-hour of sunlight left. COL Nelson seemed relieved when I reported to him that we got everyone back safe and sound. He thanked me for getting it done. I added, "Sir, the group had taken Woody's truck for that Medcap. If any truck in our Motor Pool was going to have a jack, it would be his, (the Motor Sergeant's)." He acknowledged this and realized it wasn't sloppy motor pool management.

So, why wasn't there a jack in the truck if it had one when they left the 91st? 1LT Messina told me that they had left the truck unattended while they visited the provincial hospital earlier that day. Not leaving a guard with the truck was a security failure for two reasons: 1) stuff in the truck would disappear, which is probably what happened to the jack. 2) the VC had been known to have kids drop hand grenades into the fuel tanks of unattended trucks. The hand grenade pin would be pulled, and the handle would be secured with rubber bands, which would dissolve in the fuel, making for a time-release detonation.

Another reason why this breakdown could have ended in a tragedy: it occurred about three miles from the village of My Lai where an American Division unit massacred 109 civilians in March 1968. Maybe the big red cross on the sides of our trucks bought us some leniency with the local population? After all, we had a ward at the 91st for injured Vietnamese locals, plus our unofficial Medcaps in Quang Ngai offered some welcomed opportunity for medical help. We'll never know for sure, but we definitely dodged a bullet!

2. Prelude to My Vietnam

I grew up on a horse farm in Baltimore County, Maryland. My Dad bred and trained thoroughbred racehorses, mostly for the lower stakes and claiming races at tracks in Maryland, Delaware, and West Virginia. Horses, like any livestock animal, require 24/7 attention. My brothers, sisters, and I often had to tend to those in the evenings after school if Dad had not made it back from the track yet.

Like any farm, there's always some chore to do. My brothers and I had the responsibility to make the fire in the den every night in the winter. In the spring and summer, it took all day on Saturdays and half of Sunday just to cut the two acres of lawn we had with a walk-behind, rotary mower. A hill, walkways, stone walls, shrubs, and flowerbeds crisscrossed the lawn which made mowing with a riding mower essentially impossible. Weedwhackers hadn't been invented in those days.

Our farm was about nine miles outside Towson, the county seat, quite a distance before accessing a motorway. Once when I had a party for classmates in high school, they joked that they had crossed the river, Styx, when they drove across the Little Gunpowder River, the halfway point. So, it may be fair to say that I led a sheltered life through high school. But farm life does three things for a person. First, your chores help to make you strong by lifting bales of hay and buckets full of water. Second, you learn to do things that have to get done before you can go have fun. Lastly, you learn to fix things with what you have available, i.e., the "safety pins and baling wire" solutions.

When I went off to Rutgers, The State University in New Brunswick, NJ, in the Fall of 1965, I was undecided about signing up for ROTC. I was disappointed that Rutgers only offered a choice between Army and Air Force, as I was more favorable toward the Navy at the time. My lacrosse coach advised, "Why not try the first two years to see if you like it. You don't incur an obligation to go into the military until you sign up for the second two years." So, I did and chose Army ROTC.

Late in the Fall of 1965 combat activities in Vietnam escalated. The Selective Service System terminated the married man exemption and reduced the ability for graduate student exemptions two years later. There was talk of discontinuing the undergraduate student (2-S) exemption altogether, which worried a lot of us on campus. In those days, a male graduating from high school had a choice: go on to college or get drafted.

Not to waste a good opportunity, our ROTC Department made an offer to the freshman and sophomore ROTC students: "Sign up for the second two years of ROTC, now, and you'll get a 1-D deferment until you complete your studies, undergraduate and post-graduate." So, I signed up for the commitment. Remember, this was way before the draft boards instituted the lottery system which would have been a significant reconsideration, depending on my lottery number.

As my father had served with the American Field Service in Burma, and his two brothers were officers in the Navy during

World War II, I saw serving in the military as the responsible thing for every able-bodied man. At this time, the Draft would take any man over 18 after high school if they didn't go to college. If you went to a university for a degree, you'd get your draft notice shortly after your diploma unless you went on to medical or dental school or qualified for a job which was designated "in the national interest." As I preferred to serve as an officer, rather than as an enlisted man, I saw ROTC as a reasonable option. Some classmates opted for the USMC's Platoon Leader Course in their junior year which meant no classes during the academic year but two six-week summer camps at Quantico, VA.

I had been impressed with the Rutgers Ranger ROTC unit on campus. It was an extra-curricular activity which held field training exercises and seemed to have an *esprit de corps* which impressed me. The Rutgers Ranger CO my freshman year was Jack Jacobs who went on to earn the Medal of Honor. He retired at the rank of colonel and has been a military commentator for NBC in recent years. While the unflattering stereotype for ROTC officers applies to some coming on active duty, it's largely undeserved. I suspect the quality of the officer varies as much as it does in the academies.

The extra practical field training with the Rutgers Rangers was invaluable for doing well in ROTC summer camp at Indiantown Gap Military Reservation, PA. We practiced small unit patrolling at the old Camp Kilmer property adjacent to the Piscataway Campus. One memorable winter field exercise involved slaughtering chickens someone got from the Ag School. Unfortunately, these were laying hens, which didn't tenderize when cooked on a stick over an open fire. If your teeth managed to break off a chunk of meat, you chewed a long time before you could swallow it.

Some of our extra training involved trips to Fort Bragg in

Fayetteville, N.C., over spring breaks where we, "kay-dettes," were left in the charge of NCOs at the 82nd Airborne jump school refresher training course and with another group from the Raider School, which at that time, was the NCO-equivalent of the Ranger School for officers. At the parachute jump training, we learned the PLF (Parachute Landing Fall) as military parachutes descended faster than recreational chutes to lessen the hang time and vulnerability of a soldier. We finished the morning practicing exiting an aircraft on the 34-foot tower where we jumped in a harness fixed to a zipline. To pass you had to hold your exiting form when the slack ran out of the harness. When it did, you got a violent jolt, making keeping that form not so easy. I'm told you get a lesser yank when your parachute deploys in an actual jump from a perfectly good moving airplane.

At the Raider School, we ran a challenging obstacle course; repelled off a high tower and negotiated the Raider Rope Drop into a stream. Afterwards and fairly fatigued, the NCOs formed us up in ranks and had us sit on the ground. The captain in charge of the NCOs spoke about the different kinds of heat injuries and how to tell them apart. Then he said, "Sergeant Delgado, front and center." Sergeant Delgado, who came from the Dominican Republic, marched up from behind our assembled platoon, executing his turns at sharp right angles and stood before us.

Then the captain tossed him a chicken and instructed, "SGT Delegado, show these cadets how you prevent heat stroke in the field." The sergeant grabbed the chicken by his feet and head and bit through his neck. Then he put the severed neck into his mouth and proceeded to drink the chicken's blood, rich with electrolytes and protein.

With glee in his voice, the captain told SGT Delgado, "Now pass the chicken around to the kay-dettes for a drink." By the time the chicken got to me, no blood was left. FYI, in Ranger School every trainee gets their own chicken.

I did well at the six-week ROTC summer camp at Indiantown Gap, finishing third in my platoon behind a guy from Pennsylvania Military College and another from VPI (now VA Tech), both with a cadet culture similar to what Pat Conroy describes in *Lords of Discipline*. I was in good shape from playing lacrosse and felt confident in most of the instruction we received. Leadership of our platoon rotated daily but nearing the final weeks of the program I had yet to have my turn. I finally got it on the first day of the big FTX (Field Training eXercise, i.e., war game). Unfortunately for me, our platoon was going to be the weapons platoon, equipped with 81mm mortars, M-30 machine guns, and two 106 mm Recoilless Rifles, mounted on jeeps.

I say "unfortunately" because the one day I was on sick call was the day we had weapons platoon training! Weapons platoon was an area that the Rutgers Rangers, or any other regular ROTC program, wouldn't have the equipment to practice. So, I had to do a crash afternoon review of the material we'd been given. To ramp up the anxiety, the supply officer told me, "Cadet Boyce, by signing this hand receipt you are 'pecuniarily responsible' for any lost equipment. As you can see there are many little pieces of ancillary equipment for the mortars. I suggest you put them into two cardboard boxes to corral them." I took his advice and gave the two boxes to my mortar team leaders. Luckily, by the end of the first day and my leadership, we had all our stuff together to pass on to the next weapons platoon leader.

At Indiantown Gap we got to fire many weapons and weapons systems. The demonstration of an M-16 bullets exploding a melon and a gel said to be analogous to the human body made a big impression. The high velocity of those rounds did a lot of bodily damage to whomever it hit. An M-16 bullet didn't make a clean entrance and exit hole like you see in the movies. The high velocity shockwave accompanying the bullet can amputate a limb or explode a skull.

The "Combined Arms Fire" demonstration made an even bigger impression. Mortar rounds and artillery rounds, along with 106mm recoilless rifle rounds, hitting targets on a hillside left you wondering if any combatant could survive such an assault. While lying on the ground would help protect with upward explosions from mortars, it would leave you vulnerable to munitions designed to explode before impact with the ground.

I had carried a heavy course load for my four years at Rutgers due to changing my major and taking courses required to apply to medical school. However, my grades suffered to the point that I wasn't a competitive applicant to go onto medical school as I had always hoped. I could have applied to graduate school and gotten a deferment of my orders to active duty as an officer after graduation. As I was burned out from course work, I decided to get my active-duty commitment over with instead.

I still saw serving in the military as every man's responsibility, despite my high chance of going to Vietnam during my two years. It seemed that all reasonably healthy males my age were destined to go there at some point. The anti-war movement had geared up in my junior year with SDS demonstrations and men opting to flee to Canada to avoid the draft. On one of our ROTC drill days, protestors came out to insert flowers in the barrels of our M-1 rifles.

Many of my fraternity brothers who were in pursuit of serious careers — doctor, lawyer, or engineer, seemed to get a pacifist philosophy during this time. I felt their anti-Vietnam War emerging political viewpoint was a bit disingenuous. Arlo Gutherie's *Alice's*

Restaurant, the movie and the song, captured the perspective my brothers felt about the possibility of being drafted. Some hoped for a medical disability which weren't easily gotten, despite notes from family doctors. Some claimed "Conscientious Objector" status but that only meant that they'd become a medical corpsman, treating wounded in combat in Vietnam without a firearm.

Many graduates in 1968 and 1969 applied to medical and dental schools as it would delay their being inducted by at least another four years. Applications to those schools exploded, inundating admission offices. One admissions officer told me that they were getting 80 applications for every slot in their first-year class. One of my fraternity brothers, an economics major, applied. I always wondered how many doctors came out of medical and dental schools that never intended medicine as their life's work? Even though it seemed as though every healthy male was going to find his way to Vietnam in 1968-1969, I have been surprised in my high school reunions to learn that few did, a fact that still puzzles me today.

When signing up for which branch of the Army we wanted for commissioning upon graduation, we had to choose at least one combat arms branch: Infantry, Armor, Field Artillery, Air Defense Artillery and Corps of Engineers. I think I had asked for Air Defense Artillery and had put down Medical Service Corps as one of my three options. As I had done well enough in my ROTC activities and Summer Camp, I was offered the option of signing up for a Regular Army commission instead of an Army Reserve commission. I didn't opt for the RA commission as it incurred a four-year active-duty commitment; but I was surprised to learn I'd be commissioned as a Medical Service Corps lieutenant.

I married Jean, my college sweetheart, a few days before graduation and commissioning. Jean had been accepted as a graduate student in the English Department at the Univ. of Massachusetts at Amherst for the fall of 1969, so she deferred her matriculation to join me as an Army wife.

After a honeymoon trip of a couple of weeks in Europe, we packed up her car and drove from her parent's home in New Jersey to San Antonio, TX, to report for my MSC Officers Basic Course at Ft. Sam Houston at the start of July 1969. I had always heard characters in movies refer to Texas as "God's Country." Texas seemed more the country God forgot as we drove from Houston to San Antonio in the oppressive late June heat when our car overheated on the road.

MSC Officer Basic course was an introduction to the many activities carried out by MSC officers: some emergency medical procedures, learning to draw blood and give shots, pharmaceuticals, basic hospital registration procedures, medical supply channels, and paperwork, field sanitation set ups for latrines and water treatment, and a pitch to become medivac pilots. We also had guys who were degreed medical/hospital lab clinical chemists and optometrists.

A big learning experience with military service is that you get to work with people from all over the United States, with different cultural heritages, different levels of education and different economic circumstances. A perfect indicator of this hit me at the opening assembly of my MSC Officer's Basic Course. As we came into our classroom from formation and took our seats, the Ft. Sam Houston Army Band played the usual selection of rousing martial music. When the band started playing "Dixie," a bunch of guys stood at attention at their seats with their hands over their hearts. No one can argue that Daniel Decatur Emmett's song isn't a catchy tune. I grew up in Maryland, a "Border State," where you might hear it played to close out a dance on an exuberant note.

But, never had I witnessed the earnest solemness that these guys displayed at that moment. Then, incredulously, the band master said that they'd play "Yankee Doodle" and invited the northerners to stand. I don't think any did; but we all became aware that there are different ways of thinking.

My orders slated me to stay on to take the Battalion Surgeon's Assistant course after the ten-week MSC Officer Basic before reporting to my initial assignment. The BSA Course ran an extra eight weeks of more intensive medical training akin to what field medics get, but a little more. The basic level of medical treatment at that time was the Battalion Aid Station which an MD will command in the field and an MSC when the unit is out of the war zone if no MD is available. If the docs are the COs (commanding officers), MSCs are the XOs (executive officers) for the unit. The MSC is charged with "taking care of the Army stuff," while the doc is left free to focus on treating the casualties.

In conventional warfare, the Battalion Aid Station (BAS), operates from two tents, i.e., medical treatment stations, one closer to the frontline than the other. As forces advance, the one further back will move up while the other continues treating wounded coming back from the front.

In Vietnam Battalion Aid Stations were set in a secured area, e.g., a base camp or a larger fire base. However, these BAS operated mostly as first aid stations holding morning sick calls as most battlefield wounded received treatment from assigned medical corpsmen and then, helicoptered directly to an ER at a surgical or evacuation hospital.

After my coursework, I wound up at the USAMedTC (US Army Medical Training Center) at Ft. Sam as a Training Officer. USAMedTC conducted Medical Corpsman AIT (Advanced Individual Training) coursework after Basic Training for enlisted men. I spent the next eight months cycling through cadre positions of Training Officer, Executive Officer, and Commanding Officer. I got to work with a bunch of very capable NCOs, like SFC Reagen, 1SG Bannen, and 1SG Gilbert White, who advised me and the other junior officers on how to get things done in the Army bureaucracy. There were some other senior NCOs who had little respect for young junior officers. They'd wax poetic about the good old days coming up in "The Brown Shoe Army" but often had an 'angle' to play in giving out advice. Others were just coasting, keeping a low profile, not making any waves in order to get in their 20 or 30 years in order to retire on the Army pension.

At some point, I became the Commanding Officer for Training Company B-3, which had a different mission than the other training companies. Our men would train to drive trucks within USAMedTC on various errands. They volunteered for an extra three-weeks of AIT to learn how to drive trucks and spend their third week driving trucks on errands for USAMedTC. Then they'd enter another training company for their regular medical corpsman training. Most careerist officers and NCOs thought I had come through OCS, rather than ROTC, which I took as a compliment.

Every so often, USAMedTC personnel office issued a list of all the officers in the center with their start dates. It became clear as I cycled through these positions, I soon became one of the more senior 2LTs in the center. Where did all the others go? I found out when I got my orders for Vietnam that May!

The week before Jean, Lee, our 6-month-old, and I left Ft. Sam to go on leave prior to going overseas, I took the two-day pre-Vietnam training, which involved orientation on booby traps and what precautions to take when entering a Vietnamese village. The officer in charge of our training was a 1LT with severe burns to his face and upper torso. I remembered seeing him when our Battalion Surgeon's Assistant's class toured the Burn Ward at Brooke Army Hospital. He had been strapped to a Styker frame, basically a flatbed held between parallel, tubular, stainless steel rings. The bed could be turned 360° so the patient could be oriented to a vertical, a horizontal-face-up or to a horizontal-face-down position for healing. He explained he had gotten burned in a fire fight when a bullet hit a white phosphorus grenade strapped to his pack harness. Brooke had garnered a reputation for developing treatments for severe burn patients, many of which were coming out of Vietnam. Our trainer's recovery testified to its effectiveness.

After the training course and saying good-by to my staff at training company B-3[1], we drove back east to my parent's farm in Glen Arm, MD, for leave. It was a time which weighed heavily on my mind as I had to prepare for shipping out to Vietnam at the end of June. I sort of had that feeling expressed in James Darren's 1961 song, *Goodbye Cruel World*.

NOTES

1. I had an opportunity to return to Ft. Sam Houston in 1979 while on a business trip. A colleague from work had cycled through USAMedTC as an Army reserve corpsman and took an extra course to qualify as a phlebotomist. We were both blown away to see that all the WWII barracks that was housing for the four training battalions ten years earlier had been leveled and replaced with just a few off-the-ground modern dormitories. It brought home in real terms the reduction in the armed forces after the Vietnam War.

3. Good-bye Real World

I spent my couple of weeks of leave prior to shipping out at my parents' horse farm in Long Green Valley, Maryland. Many have compared this part of Maryland with the scenic countryside of England with a mix of gently rolling hills and woodlands. Our farming neighbors grew vegetables and animal feed crops. So, a horse farm was a bit of an outlier in our area.

When my parents got the farm in 1957, only a tom cat with a single sabretooth came with it. After two female strays arrived the next year, we got a lesson in feline breeding. Now in 1970, about thirty cats and kittens commandeered the back porch by the kitchen door at mealtimes. A fury of fur would crash into the kitchen and then recede like a wave at the beach when Mom would open the door to take the big pan of Purina Dog Chow and calf milk replacer out to set it on the back walk. It was bedlam but my father had no problems with rats in the barn.

In preparation some Army friends had advised taking extra underwear, so Jean helped me dye what I had olive green with Rit Dye. The shade didn't exactly match the Army-issued undershirts, but it was close enough, if I was in a field unit. White tee shirts aren't good camouflage in the jungle.

Where my family, Jean, and my son, Lee[1], would live while I was overseas still needed to be resolved. While Mom offered that Jean and Lee could stay at the farm, Jean declined. She told me, "I don't feel comfortable living out here in the country." (Jean, a city girl, from Fords, NJ, grew up in a busy suburb with no pets. Driving 20-30 minutes to the nearest supermarket, movie theater, or museum was unimaginable.) "Neither do I see myself staying with my folks for any extended period. Instead, I think I'll activate my acceptance at U. Mass."

This plan of action worked for me; so, I set up for most of my Army pay to go directly to her with just a small amount for me for incidentals while in Vietnam. I was happy that Jean would be at U. Mass doing what she had planned to do. She'd be at home in a college town with all the intellectual stimulation and discussions with department colleagues she lacked in our year in San Antonio. We made a few trips down to Ft. Holabird in Baltimore to stock up on health and beauty aids for the next year for Jean and Lee and for me to get a GI haircut before leaving.

Our relationship had become a bit strained with my assignment at USAMedTC as it was very time consuming, and she and Lee were home alone most of any day. While she had activities and friends through the women's groups at Ft. Sam, it wasn't the same as having her husband home. I usually left the house before she and Lee were up; but got home around suppertime unless it was my time to supervise evening chow in the mess hall. She learned to accept this along with the other Army wives she'd met. They all shared the same situation. Acceptance doesn't mean she liked it. Now she would face a year of single parenting and trying to manage her studies as a graduate student in English.

Probably, as with many soldiers prior to deployment, the waiting time to ship out brought many serious questions to mind.

What would my assignment be like in-country? How much active combat would I be in or near? As I had trained as a Battalion Surgeon's Assistant, what division would I be assigned to? What were my chances of coming back in one piece or not at all? As I'm more of an introvert, this didn't make me a fun guy to be around in those last weeks of June 1970.

When the day came to fly out to the west coast to Travis AFB, I went to say good-by to my dad who was training his thoroughbreds at a nearby facility. I believe his British army unit had been under-siege by the Japanese, near Kohima in Burma; so, I valued his advice as I left for overseas. I asked, "Pop, do you have any advice for me?"

His reply, "Don't accept any wooden nickels." Not very philosophical or useful advice! I had expected something like, "Don't ever volunteer for anything." Or, "Keep your head down." To this day I am in wonder at his response.

I felt I had matured through college and spent most of a year as "head of my own (training) company" as Army ads in those days offered recruits. Yet, I was only 23 and maybe Dad recognized my inexperience with the world and going to war. Or maybe, he was just confounded with having to send his oldest off to Vietnam and remembering the risks he faced in Burma. That said, I still find his advice humorous and wish he was still around to clarify it for me.

Jean and Mom drove me down to Friendship Airport[2] to see me off on my first leg. It was a typical Maryland June day: temperatures between 85-95 degrees and humidity over 85%. You always feel like a wet dishrag in the summers in the Maryland-Washington, DC, area. The high humidity made the sky hazy so I can't say it was a beautiful day to fly. While the day might qualify as one of *Those Lazy-Hazy-Crazy Days of Summer* in the Nat King Cole song, the Maryland mugginess steams any lightheartedness out of a person if the solemness of deploying to a war zone didn't do that already.

I boarded the plane, probably a TWA flight, in my summer-weight khakis. For the first time in my life, I felt like the "soldier boy" in the Shirelle's 1962 song of the same name. I was facing a year without the comfort of my wife and son, friends, and extended family. How would I make it through the next twelve months?

I think I may have changed planes in Chicago before flying on to San Francisco. It was mid-afternoon when I arrived at SFO and took a taxi or a military shuttle bus out to Travis AFB where I was due to board the plane to Vietnam the next morning. When I checked in on base and looked to get a BOQ room for the night, I was told none were available. A clerk told me I could layout in a lounge room to get some shut eye. I wound up sharing it with a Chinook pilot, warrant officer, and two women Army nurses. We basically slept on the floor without blankets or pillows. It sufficed but certainly, substandard!

The next morning, we went to the departure area, checked in, waited, and finally went through the glass doors to a fenced in area outside. Some wives accompanied their departing husbands. The wife of another young warrant officer pilot standing next to me was getting in her last passionate kisses before seeing him off. I thought how different my send-off had been, but I wasn't sure which was better in the long run. Jean might have given me similar, passionate kisses had Mom not been right there!

Finally, we boarded a Trans International Airlines (TIA) charter flight that would eventually, take us to Bien Hoa Air Base outside Saigon. Our plane, a big (at that time) DC-8 soon filled with soldiers, like me, going solo off to war. Our somber mood reflected that most of us didn't know what to expect. I'm sure some were some second-tour guys, but I don't think they were evident outside of their rank and what insignias they had on their uniforms. I'm glad that deployments to war zones today are done by whole units and how the mood probably is a whole lot better, maybe like a sports team on an away-game trip.

I nicknamed our flight route "The WWII Battles History Tour." First, we landed at Honolulu, to refuel. Then, we continued to Wake Island and Subic Bay, in the Philippines. At some point we flew over Midway Island. Twenty-seven hours later we landed at Bien Hoa Air Base at night.

We boarded green buses with heavy, steel mesh screens over the windows to protect from grenades being thrown in. We were told that while we were in a US military reservation, occasionally insurgents get in and cause havoc. The officers on the bus got off at the transient officers' BOQ, two-story, multi-room structures with about four bunks in each room. I found a bunk and sacked out until the morning, exhausted but wondered what tomorrow would bring?

NOTES

1. Lee was born at Brooke Army Hospital in 1969 at a total cost to us of $7.50, which was the cost of Jean's meals while in the maternity ward.

2. Friendship International Airport was renamed Baltimore-Washington International Airport (BWI) in 1971

4. In-processing at Long Binh

When I awoke that first morning, the acrid smell of "burn out la-trines" assaulted my nostrils, just the opposite of that feeling in The Rascal's song, *Beautiful Morning*. Running water was not avail-able in many military areas and the potable water was reserved for drinking and meal preparations. For toileting, many GIs used outhouses where a lower third of a steel drum collected the feces and urine. Once a day someone, called a "burner," would pull the drum out, add diesel fuel to the contents and set fire to it until all was gone. Not pretty, but effective without city sewers.

With daybreak, I could see that our BOQ was situated on a dusty road surrounded by low tin-roofed buildings and trees that I'd never seen growing up in the Mid-Atlantic states. A deuce and a half truck sat outside our building. It was outfitted to shuttle soldiers around Long Binh, the largest US military installation in the world outside the USA. I snapped a photo with a disposable camera from the balcony across from my bunk room to send home when/if I could get it developed. I did wonder how Jean and Lee were getting along at the farm and how long she would stay before going to see her parents in Fords and then onto Amherst, MA.

The deuce and a half trucked us over to the supply station later that morning to pick up our issue of jungle fatigues, boots, and a duffle bag. Just like what we saw in old WWII movies: big building, many tables with supplies, lines of GIs waiting to pick up what impatient supply personnel handed out. It worked smoothly, and we reboarded a deuce-and-a-half to go back to the transient officers BOQ to wait for our assignments.

On the drive back, I remember seeing SFC Okyama, who worked with me at USAMedTC, walking with others in the transient enlisted men's area. I wondered how he felt to make a return trip to Vietnam; wasn't one tour enough? Today, I'm amazed that some soldiers have spent three, four, and five tours to the Mideast war zones. I understand that the tours are shorter, but the repeat process must take its toll on one's mind, not to mention their families at home.

Much later in my assignment, I met a SSGT at an Americal Division's in-country orientation class who was starting his *fourth* tour in Vietnam. He explained that he didn't respond well in stateside assignments or his last assignment in West Germany. He couldn't tolerate the "Mickey Mouse/Chicken Shit Rules" in that environment. He'd get into trouble, and to avoid a court-martial, he'd re-up for another tour in Vietnam. Unbelievable! Or was this one manifestation of what we now call PTSD, what Kathryn Bigelow's movie, *The Hurt Locker*, portrays with a demolitions officer in Iraq?

Later that morning, I met with the MSC assignment officer who asked, "Do you have any assignment preferences?" I thought this question a bit unusual as I expected I'd be told what my assignment would be without any input from me.

Before leaving for Vietnam, Jean (and my mother) sternly told me, "Don, I don't want you to go looking for trouble/combat if you don't have to. I want you coming home."

I replied, "I'll only request assignment with the 101st to be with Tommy." Tommy was my cousin and almost like a brother to me. He landed in-country about 3-4 months before me, and my uncle told me he "was out in the shit."

So, I replied, "I'd like to go to the 101st Airborne in Phu Bai to be with my cousin."

He said, "I don't have any MSC vacancies there; but I have an opening in the 7th Cavalry Airmobile Regiment if you're interested." I declined that posting because the chopper pilot I shared the lounge room overnight at Travis AFB said the 7th Cav was the one unit he'd didn't want. He said that they were known to "take too many (unnecessary) chances."

So, I accepted a hospital unit assignment. He told me, "You'll be going to the 67th Medical Group, headquartered in Da Nang, and they would make your unit assignment." The 67th Med Group had responsibility for the non-divisional medical care units in I & II Corp (northern half of South Vietnam).

Later that afternoon, I boarded a C-130 cargo plane along with about 50 men and the two nurses I'd met at Travis for the plane ride up country. Unfortunately, there were no seats on this C-130 so everyone had to sit on the metal pallet floor of the cargo bay. Not the most comfortable and not the safest if we had to make a rough landing!

After a stop or two to let off some soldiers at Nha Trang and Cam Rahn Bay, we landed at Da Nang AFB after dark. A MAJ Pedersen, who handled personnel assignments for the 67th Med Group welcomed the nurses and me. He got us something to eat, had us shown to overnight bunks, and said we'd meet in the morning to finalize our assignment. I was shown to a fortified sea hut occupied by other MSC officers assigned to the 95th Evac Hospital at China Beach.

We breakfasted in a superlative mess hall run by the Navy. The walls were paneled in big squares of dark stained and grooved plywood with the grooves alternating direction between adjacent panels. The roof was high peaked, cathedral like, versus the typical low ceiling in Army mess halls. The tables displayed center pieces of doves made from artfully slicing an apple. Afterwards, MAJ. Pedersen informed me, "You'll going to the 91st Evac Hospital in Chu Lai about 60 miles south of here." He added, "LTC (Joe) Gipson, your XO, is up for the day and you'll travel together down to the 91st."

Upon meeting him, LTC Gipson appeared an upbeat extrovert and exuded an infectious positive energy. Instinctively, I felt he would be a good guy to work for and at no time for the few months I worked for him had my guts betrayed me. He was like the good coaches I had in high school and college. He valued the totality of the unit team and how it worked together, something his successor seemed not to do.

Before we would catch our helicopter ride back to Chu Lai, LTC Gipson had to make two stops. One was at an ARVN (Army of the Republic of *south* Vietnam) HQ of some sort to drop off some paperwork. I stayed in the jeep while he did this. The building he went into was solid masonry with a high wall and two ARVN guards at the entrance.

Once he had finished his business, he wanted to stop by the PX at China Beach. In contrast to the ARVN HQ, these buildings were typical Army structures of wood-frame construction with corrugated metal roofing. While LTC Gipson was inside, I waited outside in the jeep to take in the beach scene. It looked like any other beach I'd ever been to, except populated with only/mostly guys. At that time, China Beach was an in-country R&R (Rest and Relaxation) location for our troops for short breaks from active combat. The out-of-country R&R locations of Honolulu, Taipei, Bangkok, Sidney, and Hong Kong served for longer breaks of a week.

The 95th Evac Hospital sat next to China Beach. One of the nurses I came up country with remained there. The other nurse was going to the 27th Surgical (Surg) Hospital, also in Chu Lai. She flew down in the same UH-1 (Huey) helicopter as LTC Gipson and me. It was a beautiful sunny day and we had great views through the open doors. I was happy for the seat belt when the helicopter banked in a turn: if you'd happen to slide off your seat, it was curtains[1]. I snapped a photo of my boot toe at the edge of the doorway and the river below with V-shaped structures used to corral fish for harvesting.

We landed on the 91st's helipad, next to the hospital's Emergency Room. It overlooked the South China Sea as it sat on an 80-100 foot cliff. The early afternoon sun beat down and the heat wafted up from the helipad tarmac. I slipped on my new aviator Ray-Ban sunglasses to make the trip with my duffle to the door of the ER. While I felt the heat, I recognized that the sea breezes would keep our location a little cooler than the units further inland.

The 91st Evac Hospital[2], itself, was mostly a series of about 20 corrugated metal Quonset huts linked by a covered boardwalk. Within these structures housed the ORs, pathology labs, surgical and disease recovery wards, dentist and optometrist offices, and the unit orderly room. Other buildings on-site included: metal Butler buildings housing the warehouse, laundry, and motor pool; wood-framed sea huts housing for officers and senior NCOs; two-story, wood-framed barracks for enlisted men; a mess hall; and two, two-story, motel-like structures of single rooms for senior doctors, nurses, and the Red Cross women, known as "Donut Dollies."

As I took in the scene of where I'd spend the next year, I looked forward to meeting the people I'd be working with. Coming from the special environment of a training company to a regular, active working Army unit would require some adjustment. As a training company CO, I was the 'top dog' of 150 men, whereas in an Evac Hospital, I'd be a staff manager off to the side of the line reporting structure.

NOTES

1. A month or two after arriving at the 91st Evac, the order came down that on "milk run"/non-combat flights the Huey doors were to remain closed while flying because of accidents.

2. The hospital was rated as having a 300-bed capacity with the mission to treat serious traumatic injuries and to either cure them or stabilize them sufficiently so that the wounded could be evacuated to Yokohama.

5. No Fourth of July Surprise

I had arrived on July 4th and the ER was relatively quiet. Nurses and corpsmen busily restocked supplies and finished dressing the wounds of a soldier. Exiting the ER, I walked down the covered boardwalk past the OR buildings, pathology lab, back-up generator and numerous wards for surgical and medical patients. About midway, the boardwalk branched left toward the Admin Company orderly room and down past the chapel to the Red Cross building where the "Donut Dollies" offered a game room and the overseas telephone for making calls back to family in the US.

The last Quonset hut on the left after passing more surgical recovery and the medical patient wards functioned as the hospital's main orderly room with offices for the CO, XO, Adjutant, and Sergeant Major. Entering the orderly room, I recognized a familiar face, 1LT Warren Brennan, a fellow training company CO at USMedTC. He had arrived about a month or two before me. Warren was the Adjutant and warmly welcomed me to the 91st. If memory serves me right, Warren came from Pennsylvania and had been a graduate school teaching assistant for either undergraduate or graduate level biochemistry. He, along with a lot of the other junior officers I worked with, came out of the same classes at OCS.

As it was the 4th of July, the hayseed in me expected that the VC might celebrate the occasion with a rocket attack as an ironic commemoration of the US's independence. I had the feeling expressed in Creedence Clearwater Revival's *Bad Moon Rising*. I told Warren of my apprehension and he chuckled, saying, "Not to worry. We're having a cookout tonight to celebrate!"

Warren acknowledged that Chu Lai experienced the rare, 122 mm-rocket attacks from the VC but that the basecamp was so large with a lot of empty space that hitting a specific target was just a chance[1,2]. He pointed out the col in the mountains in the distance and called it the "rocket pocket" from where most of the rockets were fired. He admitted that rockets aimed toward the Americal HQ area might fall short and hit the 91st Evac.

As I was trying to grasp this concept, Warren said that he'd show me to my hooch, a 16'x32' wood-frame building with a corrugated metal roof. Officially, it was a sea hut, but everyone called it a hooch. We walked back to the road that ran from the main hospital toward the sea. Along both sides were the hooches for junior officers and senior NCOs. At the road's end were the 2-story private rooms for senior, field-grade doctors, and the nurses.

Warren explained that some of the hooches had been enclosed and had A/C. Unfortunately, the one I was assigned to was still open. The hooches resembled the type of building you'd see at a sleepover, summer camp for kids: wood siding 2/3rds of the wall, open screening for the rest and plywood flaps to cover the opening during heavy rains. The hooch was surrounded by a three to four-foot wall of sandbags as protection from shrapnel. Each hooch held four Army cots and up-right metal lockers for their occupants' belongings. I made up my cot with the issued sheets and set up an oscillating desk fan to blow air on me during the night. At night our lights inside the hooch would attract insects to our screens and small, flesh-colored lizards would perch on the screens looking to snag the insects.

Warren bunked in the hooch next to mine which was split in half with both sides having an A/C unit. He shared his half with CPT Dick Lamster who was the hospital's supply officer, our S-4. The walls of their hooch were paneled with pine plywood that had been scorched with a blow torch to accentuate the grain and then varnished. Dick had an electric fry pan that he used mostly to cook Chef Boyardee pizzas that he made from the mix kits his family mailed to him. Dick hailed from South Dakota and had been a physical education graduate of Univ. of South Dakota and planned to become a gym teacher when he got out of the service. One oddity of the 91st Evac is that we had about four other officers from South Dakota. Three MSC officers and a male nurse all from the Pierre area in the same unit, in Vietnam at the same time? How weird was that?

Dave Lynn, the Admin Company CO, and Elmo Vinas, the Registrar, resided in a hooch or two on the other side of my new home. While their paneling was less deluxe, they, too, had A/C. Dave was from somewhere in the Mid-Atlantic and Elmo was raised in Texas. Dave would DEROS soon and was looking forward to being with his fiancé again. Elmo, a sandy-haired and affable guy, had an outgoing personality and friendliness that would make him a very good salesmen in the civilian world.

Warren left me to get my things stowed. He said he'd return in a little while to take me to the hospital cookout for dinner. It was held in the space between the two housing units for senior doctors and nurses and our Officer's Club. My jaw dropped as we walked into the cookout area. A jeep trailer, parked down by the O-Club was filled with sodas and beers on ice. The mess sergeant was cooking hamburgers and hot dogs on a grill made from a

55-gal steel drum cut in half. The buns for the burgers and dogs had been baked in the mess hall and were the tastiest I've ever had. A long table with French fries, baked beans, coleslaw, and condiments completed the dinner fare.

Soon, a 4-piece band set-up and started to play. The guys came from Americal Special Services and had been playing together for the better part of a year, and it showed. They'd go out to the firebases to provide some entertainment along with the Red Cross women bringing books and toiletries. One of their numbers included Country Joe and the Fish's *I Feel Like I'm Fixin' to Die Rag*. The sentiment in this song resonated with the docs, as most had been drafted and they would treat the traumatic injuries of the unpopular war every day.

While we were eating our food, Warren took me to the gap between a doctors' hooch and the O-Club to look out across the bay at the extinct volcano jutting out at the other end. The scene resembled pictures of Diamondhead in Honolulu with a major exception: cobra gunships firing down red tracer bullets and dodging green tracers coming up at them. The scene was a bit surreal.

My family made me promise to write them once I got to my unit in Vietnam to let them know where I wound up. When I wrote them about my first day at the 91st Evac, my Mom's reply letter begged me to tell them the truth about where I really was. She surely assumed that I had stepped through the Looking Glass and off the Deep End!

NOTES:

1. Later in my assignment I saw the hole in the roof of the Quonset hut for the

34

medical patient ward. It was where a piece of shrapnel from a nearby rocket hit came through and killed the nurse on duty at that time.

2. "It was the morning of June 8, 1969, and 1st Lt. Sharon Lane, a U.S. Army nurse, was finishing an overnight shift at the 312th Evacuation Hospital in Chu Lai, South Vietnam, when the hospital came under enemy fire....With her death, Lane became the only U.S. military nurse killed by enemy fire in the Vietnam War." https://www.jbsa.mil/News/News/Article/1740278/ new-amedd-museum-exhibit-honors-only-us-nurse-killed-by-enemy-fire-in-vietnam/#:~:text=It%20was%20the%20morning%20of,hospital%20came%20 under%20enemy%20fire.&text=With%20her%20death%2C%20Lane%20 became,fire%20in%20the%20Vietnam%20War.

6. First Americal PX Visit

The next day Warren took me over to the Americal PX, the main PX for Chu Lai, which was just outside our compound gates. First order of business was to visit the Korean tailors to get my insignia sewn on my jungle fatigues. Because we were in the rear, we wore our black rank insignia on our lapel. (The Army was turning away from brass/silver rank and branch insignia to all matte black). A guy operating a zigzag sewing machine deftly embroidered my name, by hand, on olive-drab, cloth tape. Then he sewed on my name tags, lapel insignia, and USARV arm patch onto my fatigues along with the big unit, maroon and white patch for the 91st Evac over my right breast pocket.

As in any PX on an Army post, you could get cases of beer and soda, hard liquor, cameras, and jewelry among other necessities. Adjoining it was the barbershop staffed with Vietnamese barbers who would use an electric massager on your neck and shoulders after cutting your hair. They had been ordered not to provide the "cervical snap," a customary Vietnamese practice. Too many GIs had come away with neck issues when the barbers quickly jerk/twist the customer's head to one side at the end of the massage. Later on, I had heard that some GIs got traditional body massages at another section but I never availed myself of those services.

Cases of beer and soda were about the same price, both under $3/case. I picked up a quart of Bacardi rum for $1.80 and a case of Coke for the hooch. (Before taking my home leave to the US, I bought a sapphire "dinner ring" for Jean at the jewelry counter.)

Many soldiers picked up reel-to-reel tape decks, turntables, stereo amplifier-tuners, and speakers at this PX or ordered them through PACEX out of Hong Kong. Long before our kids were downloading mixtapes on CDs at college, we were copying LPs onto reel-to-reel tapes[1] in Vietnam. Certainly, the Vietnam War generated a generation of discerning audiophiles through the easy access to good audio equipment. One corpsman told me that his set up allowed him to hear higher quality sound compared to the stereo record players most people had had growing up in the US.

I was grateful for Warren's taking time to what companies now call "on boarding" me to the 91st and Chu Lai. While I still felt like an FNG, I wasn't treated like a rookie at pre-season camp for a professional sports team where some degree of initiation/hazing occurs.

––––––––

NOTES:

1. Cassette tapes hadn't made it big in Vietnam yet. Pre-recorded cassettes only started to appear in the US in 1966. The first cassette tape I ever saw belonged to my dispatcher, James Radford. They offered a handy compactness that the forerunner, 8-track, did not.

Americal PX source of many necessities.

Americal PX and helipad.

7. 91st Evac Hosp Semi-Mobile Site

The 91st Evac was one of two hospitals in Chu Lai. The 27th Surgical Hospital Semi-mobile was a few miles inland. As the name suggests, it only did surgeries and did not have medical wards for patients suffering from diseases, like malaria, dysentery, hepatitis, chronic STDs and dengue fever.

Our unit was situated atop an 80–100 foot bluff with a view of the main beach, tanker port, and an extinct volcano, resembling Diamond Head in Honolulu. A chain of low-level mountains to our south made for a pretty, scenic location if not for the military complex that occupied the area. Someone said that this area had been a beach getaway for the colonial Chinese[1] and, also by the colonial French[2]. To many of us at the 91st Evac, we could easily imagine hotels springing up after the war along the beaches in Chu Lai[3]. The benefit from our location was the heat-tempering sea breezes we'd get in the summer/dry season. I'm not sure whether these reached the 27th Surg a few miles away.

Still, local fishermen would depart in late afternoon from the main beach in LRBs (Little Round Boats) made of reeds with a tarred bottom to tend fishing nets as a group. Support units along the beachline had guard towers on the lookout at night for any faux-fishermen/VC trying to come ashore before dawn.

I'm told that Chu Lai is not a Vietnamese name, rather a Chinese one. Apparently, a U.S. Marine general gave this name to the base camp area when they first set it up. Originally, the site started as the hospital for the 1st Marine Battalion. The Army took it over in 1968, replacing it with the 312th Evac, a reserve unit out of Winston-Salem, NC, for a year of service. (We always wondered what went through the minds of the men in the 312th when they got orders to ship out to Vietnam. They had worked so hard to get into a reserve Army unit to avoid going to Vietnam!) In 1969, the Army replaced them with the 91st Evac Hosp, moving it up from its previous location in Tuy Hoa, further south on the coast between Qui Nhon and Nha Trang.

Besides the bluff overlooking the South China Sea, our compound was hemmed in by an outdoor amphitheater built for the 1967 Bob Hope show (used in 1968 and 1969) to the north, the Chu Lai PX, the Americal HQ to the west, and a transportation unit to the south.

At the entrance to our compound stood a big water tank which supplied the hospital and gave running water to the showers, toilets, and sinks located in the different living areas. We knew this was a big luxury, but a necessity for hospital sanitation. Stateside we had seen film clips of GIs washing up in makeshift, outdoor showers with sun-heated water streaming from a 5-gallon tin container or a 55-gal drum.

Electrical service to the hospital meant that we had lighting and receptacles for stereos, fans, and A/Cs in the living spaces. The electrical power was generated by a power station a few miles away, which was operated by Philco-Ford, a civilian contractor.

Consequently, we did not have to deal with the white noise of a local generator for our electricity.

Another plus with the 91st was that we arguably had one of the best mess halls in the base camp. I make this claim based on the numerous visitors who ate there from the Americal and the national journalists in the area on assignment[4]. Our mess hall was run by a savvy career warrant officer. He had worked his way up through the enlisted ranks and his experience showed. I'd never had such a splendid Thanksgiving or Christmas dinner as those during my tour at the 91st. This is not to say my mom was a slouch when it came to these meals; she was very good. (Her sage dressing recipe still judged the best any friend or relative has had.) But the mess hall crew presented an epic array of pies and sides to accompany the turkey and stuffing.

Our little compound had its own EM- and O-Clubs for off-duty relaxation. Besides bar service there was usually a movie every night unless a traveling USO-sponsored floor show played at one of our clubs. The USO floor shows coming to the 91st clubs usually came out of Korea or the Philippines. The groups played and sang popular songs of the 60's, usually without an Asian accent, which amazed all of us.

All in all, our compound had a lot of benefits the others in Chu Lai didn't, which none of us took for granted. Despite these creature comforts, you still missed your family and friends back home. Bobby Bare's *Detroit City* with its lamented wish to return home captures that feeling. I don't think there was a night that I went to sleep in my cot that I didn't wish I was back in the States with Jean and Lee.

Your only link to your people was APO mail, now called "snail mail," and the Red Cross phone which would cost your recipient $2/minute on a collect call with a maximum time of 10 minutes.

The 12-hour time difference between Chu Lai and the East Coast posed a timing drawback for using the Red Cross phone line: You didn't want to call at four in the afternoon!

NOTES:

1. China ruled Vietnam for 1,000 years, ending in 986 AD.
2. The French made Vietnam a colony as of 1877 and finally relinquished it in 1954 after their defeat at Dien Bien Phu by Ho Chi Minh.
3. As of 2019, the resort hotels have not come to Chu Lai. Much of the development has been industrial
4. ABC journalist, Sam Donaldson, and others were in our mess hall for breakfast one morning. They were there to cover the story about the VC over-running FB Mary Ann in March 1971.

Bob Hope Amphitheater.

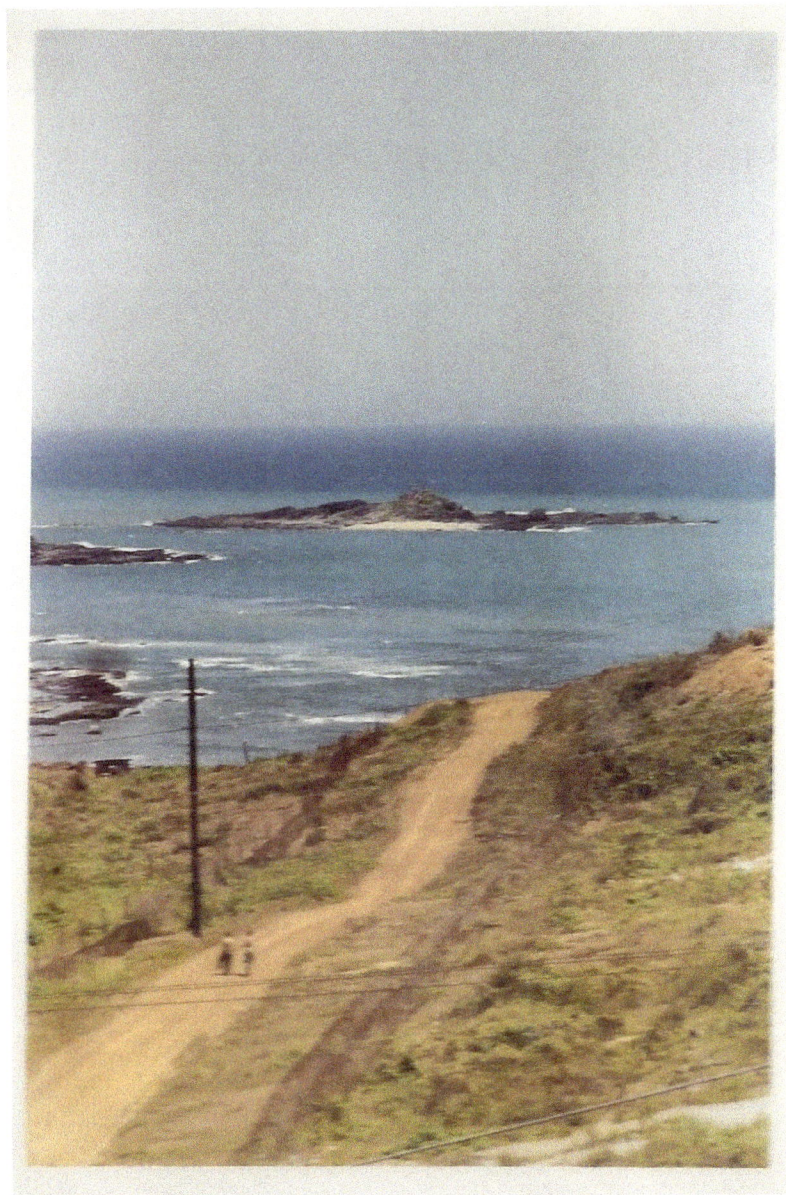

View along North Border of 91st Evac Hosp.

91st Evac Wards along North Border toward helipad..

View of east compound with orderly room, EM bar-
racks, sea huts and senior officers' & nurses' housing

Corpsmen's two-story barracks.

Covered walkway leading from Mess Hall to Doc's hooch at point.

View southward to Main Beach and 'rocket pocket.'

View to southwest to SGM's hooch and mountains.

8. OJT at the 91st Evac

MSCs do a lot of things within an Army hospital—we serve as registrars, medical supply officers, med lab officers, pharmacists, none of which I had the extra Army coursework beyond the Officer's Basic at Ft Sam or the academic credentials from university. Yet I was told by MAJ Pedersen at the 67th Med Group that I would be filling a hospital registrar's slot. However, CPT Elmo Vinas was already the 91st Evac's registrar. So that didn't happen.

I had been a training company commander at USAMedTC so LTC Gipson initially assigned me to succeed 1LT Dave Lynn as the Admin Company CO when he'd DEROS in a month or two. I held this as my primary duty for about 4-6 weeks until CPT Frank Nance arrived and he got the position and LTC Gipson moved me to be the unit's Motor Officer, reporting to CPT Dick Lamster, the S-4/Supply Officer.[1]

While I had headed a training company at Ft. Sam which trained truck drivers for USAMedTC, I knew little about vehicle maintenance, other than how to change the oil and filter and spark plugs in my car. Our unit had four to five 2-1/2-ton trucks, a.k.a. "deuce and a halfs," a dump truck, a tow truck, two ¾-utility trucks and the CO's jeep. The deuce-and-a-halfs were diesel-motored to boot, so no spark plugs, fuel injectors instead.

We had just gotten the use of part of a large, grey, metal Butler Building for our main work area which replaced the open ended, canvas tunnel that had been the only covered maintenance area. The baked red clay of our parking lot for the trucks was serviceable enough but dusty during the dry season and made for a slick, smeary surface in light rain. We had a shack for the dispatcher, another one for our spare parts and an "illegal," small, metal shipping container. This Conex container held spare parts in excess of our PLL (Prescribed Load List, our authorized stocking level).

Whenever we'd have a periodic, official IG inspection, we'd have to move the Conex container off-site before the inspectors arrived. The huge forklift at our warehouse would make the move and would have to remain off-site for the inspections as well. It had been bequeathed to the 91st by departing Navy Seabees and was not authorized equipment for an Evac Hospital.

My crew consisted of a sad sack Motor Sergeant that would soon DEROS back to the States, a mechanic, PFC John Rink, a dispatcher, PVT James Radford, and a mechanic & PLL Clerk, CPL Capps. Luckily, our incoming Motor Sergeant, Charles "Woody" Woods was very capable and was an upgrade over his predecessor. As an experienced mechanic before the Army, Woody was knowledgeable, patient, and willing to share his knowledge with his crew in a way they accepted. His upbeat and outgoing personality made him a pleasure to work with.

Woody emphasized Operator Maintenance (OM) responsibilities for the warehouse guys who drove our trucks around the base camp picking up incoming supplies. This change became the linchpin of his greatest contribution. His predecessor had been lax in OM and the trucks' conditions reflected that. Woody assigned each truck to a specific driver rather than let them take whichever was available when they needed it. This policy change gave each driver a stake in their truck.

Woody let the drivers repaint their vehicles to spruce them up. Some thought they'd sex up their truck's look by adding a little black paint to the standard olive-drab paint. A bit of natural competitiveness led to some trucks looking more like black with a greenish tinge. Although I was tempted to object, Woody convinced me to overlook the color variance in favor of the drivers improved care of their vehicles.

I picked up an extra duty as Beach Officer, probably a duty the Army still doesn't have an MOS code for. The year before the new commanding general of the American Division arrived in Chu Lai, there were seven drownings in the South China Sea. GIs from the units bordering the cove at Chu Lai swam at any convenient place and not at the main beach staffed with lifeguards. Unfortunately, strong rip currents in the cove led to those drownings. Consequently, the commanding general proclaimed that there would be only seven authorized beaches staffed with lifeguards and rescue equipment and supervised by a Beach Officer.

Americal HQ designated the small beach at the 91st as one of the authorized beaches. Having been a camp counselor in high school conducting supervised swims and an after work surfer at a New Jersey beach during my college summers, I didn't think this add-on duty was going to be a challenging burden.

I picked up two more ancillary duties that year: Auditor of the Patient Trust Fund and TO&E Document Update project. The Patient Trust Fund is like a mini bank. It consists of the money taken from incoming injured soldiers for safekeeping when they enter the hospital for treatment, and they get it back when they discharge or transfer out. As hand calculators had not been in use in those days, my auditing consisted of reviewing and checking the math in the ledger book with pencil and paper that the ER clerk kept. Apparently, those who had the duty before me did only a perfunctory review and signed off on whatever the balance shown in the ledger.

In my review I found discrepancies and after doing the math a couple of times, it seemed as though the cash box was about $300 short. The corpsman in charge of the fund at that time was a known heroin addict, so we didn't know whether the shortfall was him siphoning off a few MPC notes, his carelessness under the influence, or due to the lax reviews of the past. Who knows, maybe it was a bit of all?

Updating the TO&E (Table of Organization and Equipment) was an interesting exercise in seeing the clash between administrative vision and the realities of operating a hospital in a war zone. The project was initiated in the spring of 1971 as US forces were looking to draw down from the great escalation during the latter part of the Johnson administration. The Army's Medical Department wanted the hospitals' TO&E revised to reflect what was really needed. COL Kenwyn Nelson, our CO, said that we probably had more staff and equipment than our TO&E which had been developed years earlier.

One glaring difference was that our unit was classified as a 'semi-mobile' evacuation hospital, usually operated under tents, or in inflatable roofed units, called MUSTs in the Vietnam era. Most hospitals in Vietnam were in permanent, Quonset huts. Secondly, all the equipment needed was supposed to be moved by the unit's trucks. There was no way that could happen given the four to five deuce-and-a-half's we had in our Motor Pool.

One benefit of this duty was that it gave me a couple of opportunities to fly up to Da Nang to work with MAJ Pedersen who was consolidating the documents from the other hospitals in the 67th Med Group. He acknowledged the disparity between what was probably needed and what the outdated documents authorized. I was uncomfortable that we didn't have any of the surgeons working on this project as their knowledge of the needs of the ORs, ER, and other medical treatment facilities would be better at arriving at a more realistic staffing and equipment level.

I never saw the completed updated TO&E as MAJ Pedersen had to consolidate the input from the other Evac hospitals in the 67th Med Group's area. I wonder to this day…did the final document reflect the real needs or a politically pressured fantasy? The process was very much like budgeting processes I saw later in my business life. That is, company politics or Finance Dept. rules discouraged a true picture of what a company needed to accomplish its goals. Just foolhardy, gaming the business metrics to appeal to investors instead of gearing up to serve and grow your customer base.

I embraced my new job and tasks with enthusiasm to learn something new. This attitude served me well later in graduate school and in business life where often I had to absorb new technologies in getting work done. Today many of us can look back on how we've adjusted to the new computer devices and software we've had to learn since the 1970s.

NOTES:

1. A few weeks after arriving at the 91st Evac, I was at an Americal Officer's Club show and met their personnel officer who was complaining that he'd just had to assign an incoming, registrar trained, MSC officer to be a Battalion Surgeon's Assistant to one of their brigades. An ironic, yet all too common occurrence in matching the people you have to the jobs you need done in any organization. Keeping my promise to Jean, I didn't volunteer to switch!

9. Don and Jim Improve Their Hooch

While the openness of the hooch was good for air flow, nights were still too warm for a recuperative sleep. It brought back memories of trying to sleep in my aunt's apartment in NYC on a late June night. Her townhouse in Greenwich Village had no air conditioning other than an open second-story window to her street. The concrete and surrounding buildings acted as a heat sink during the day and a radiator at night. Noise from trucks making night deliveries across the street below kept this country boy from getting a good night's sleep. Basically, I was trying to sleep under conditions described in the Lovin' Spoonful song, *Summer in the City*, only we were in Chu Lai.

In a futile effort to better the sleeping conditions, everyone had an oscillating desk fan by their beds to provide some cooling when they tried to sleep. We were given a nylon poncho liner as a blanket which would be needed during the cooler monsoon season. The only improvement our hooch had was a mini refrigerator, the kind we see in college dorm rooms today. We'd keep it stocked with beer and sodas we'd pick up at the Americal PX.

The hooch was meant to house four officers, each having a corner to make our own with our cot and an upright metal locker for clothes. One occupant when I arrived was a junior doctor who returned to the States the day after my arrival. 2LT Marty Brown arrived a day or two after me. Later we were joined by CPT Jim Robbins, a nurse. So, for the next couple of months, it was just the three of us.

Jim and I shared some of the same regrets from college, despite our diverse backgrounds. He hailed from Oklahoma, a state I have yet to set foot in, and claimed some Cherokee heritage. He was a few years older than me and had been in the Army as a corpsman and had been promoted to SSGT prior to leaving the Army and attending nursing school. He had a wife and three young kids back in the States. His GI Bill benefits started to run out at the beginning of his last year of earning his BSN degree. So, needing the funds, he signed up for an Army Nurse Corps (ANC) scholarship which required going back in on active duty, as an officer. His previous service years qualified him to start as a captain while other recent graduates started as second lieutenants.

Since he found himself in Vietnam (and rooming with an East Coaster?) he was kicking himself for not making more of an effort to find alternative sources of financial support. (Ironically, looking to upgrade his skills for a higher salary, Jim signed up for nurse anesthetist training at the end of his tour. He said that after he completed that active-duty commitment, he'd go onto civilian jobs. I wonder if he really did, or whether he wound up doing the 20 years in the Army?)

Rooming with Jim was an education in many things. One was giving me some insight as to what the doctors and nurses faced every day. Being out in the motor pool I had little first-hand knowledge of what was going on in the medical treatment areas. Like other incoming nurses, Jim started on a medical ward, then worked the ER and, later, took care of patients on surgical wards.

After the heavy load of traumatic injuries in the ER, going to the surgical care wards was a relief.

Jim's second influence on me was country music. Before meeting Jim, most of my music listening came from Top-40 AM stations, e.g., WCAO in Baltimore and WABC in New York with "Cousin Brucie" Morrow. Most rock and roll music broadcasted from AM stations as FM station listening hadn't come into its own. That said, I did own some classical and folk music records from my high school years. At Rutgers, our fraternity parties played rock and soul music like the Stones', The Temptation's and Smokey Robinson and the Miracles. While some people might view my taste as diverse, it lacked an appreciation for country music, outside of crossover hits like Bobbie Gentry's *Ode to Billie Joe*. The closest I came to Jim's music was Creedence Clearwater Revival and Elvis Presley. Jim introduced me to Merle Haggard's tribute album to Jimmy Rogers, *Same Train, A Different Time,* and his latest hit, *Okie from Muskogee*. Jim's collection also contained Johnny Cash's *At Folsom Prison* album, Jeannie C. Riley's *Harper Valley PTA* and a Billie Jo Spears number or two. Once when I asked how he could like "that music," Jim replied in his Oklahoman draw, "Boyce, that's the voice of Uh-muricah speaking." All I can say, it grew on me, and I learned after leaving Vietnam, I could listen to country music radio stations longer than the Top 40 stations. Today, my car's radio is either on *Willie's Roadhouse* for the classical country voices or *Prime Country* featuring artists like George Strait, Alan Jackson, and Janie Fricke.

Jim and I didn't like having to try to sleep in the heat at night with an oscillating fan laboring to keep us cooler. We were motivated to enclose our hooch and install an A/C unit like our neighbors. We began reclaiming the plywood from the shipping crates the medical supplies came in for the 91st. The dimensions of these crates weren't uniform, so the pieces of plywood we turned into paneling for the inside of our hooch made for a patchwork quilt look. Removing the 1" x 2" strips of wood from the plywood was tedious and had us sweating profusely in the early evenings when we worked.

As Marty opted out of this endeavor, Jim and I decided to panel just our half of the hooch, which reduced the amount of reclaim work we had before us. Since the crate plywood came from the Philippines, the outer veneer was mahogany! We had a few pieces left over from our paneling which I used to make a rudimentary desk next to my bunk. After varnishing it with polyurethane, the beauty of the wood shone through[1]. Jim made a small bar with more leftover plywood. It looked sharp once he finished it. Since our hooch was not a social gathering point, I never understood Jim's motivation for building it.

After we finished the last of the paneling, Jim found an A/C unit from a departing Americal guy. How he found out about it, I never knew. The only problem was that the unit required a 240-volt electrical line. Not to worry! One of the warehouse guys had electrician's skills and, he, somehow, added a second 120-volt line to the existing receptacle, upgraded the plug for a 3-pole plug and we were in business. The A/C unit was rated at 24,000 BTU, all for a 16' x 16'-foot room and was very effective in cooling our area, despite no insulation within the wall.

Despite our different backgrounds, Jim and I saw the value of 'sweat equity' in improving our living conditions. Our work paid off in giving us a tolerable living space.

NOTES:

1.   I think this little project initiated my interest in woodworking to make mortise

and tenon joined tables, cabinets, and shelving. The beauty of good wood coated in clear varnish to allow its beauty to shine through never gets old.

Our hooch and residence for 11 months and 23 days.

CPT Jim Robbins on the way to work.

CPT Jim Robbins and author at Jim's new bar.

Author's desk and bunk area.

10. Off-Duty Life at a S*M*A*S*H

*M*A*S*H*, the movie, debuted in March 1970. I saw it in April/ May of that year just before leaving Ft. Sam to go on leave before Vietnam. While the 91st was an Evac hospital, it and the 27th Surg were considered "Semi-mobile" units even though we treated the sick and wounded in fixed Quonset hut buildings. To be "semi-mobile" we would have MUST units, where the treatment rooms had inflatable walls, like rafts. One of the first Army hospitals in Vietnam did have MUST units but after a year were replaced with Quonset huts. So, had the movie been made about medical units in the Vietnam War, would the producers have called it, S*M*A*S*H?

Regardless of these silly details, life within the 91st had an uncanny resemblance to the movie. One direct comparison was that two of our docs, one a neurosurgeon, had an unauthorized jeep for their personal use. Unlike the movie, they didn't steal it; but had traded a sergeant a box of penicillin for it! Another doc had hand-receipted a powerboat and water skis from the NCOIC of the American Division's Special Services unit. When the weather and water conditions were calm enough, some docs and nurses waterskied out in the bay/cove[1].

The doctors, nurses, and corpsmen treated the traumatic injured coming off the battlefield by Medivac helicopters. The evacuation time from the battlefield to our ER was very fast, said to be no more than about 20-30 minutes. This meant that more wounded soldiers survived with lifelong disabilities whereas they would have probably died enroute to a doctor in an ambulance during WWII and the Korean Conflict[2].

While the incoming casualties flowed and ebbed, the docs and nurses were always debriding wounds, cauterizing bleeders, stitching organs and skin back together, changing dressing, and caring for patients on the mend, or preparing them for evacuation to Yokohama, Japan. Understandably, the docs, nurses, and corpsmen who did this work often partied hard. A couple of the docs' hooches had the reputation of being the places for off-duty parties. (Cue the M*A*S*H theme song, *Suicide Is Painless!*)

Like M*A*S*H we usually had a movie at both our EM- and O-Clubs every night. It was surreal for me to watch the *Woodstock* documentary in early 1971. Before I graduated from Rutgers, I had heard some of my fraternity brothers talking about a big concert that some were hoping to attend that summer. After seeing the chaos, rain, and mud in that movie, I was happy to have been at Ft Sam in Officer Basic when it happened. Still, I enjoyed seeing Richie Havens perform as well as Jimi Hendrix, a former member of the 82nd Airborne Division, play his psychedelic guitar rendition of the *Star Spangled Banner*.

Unlike M*A*S*H, we had a small beach below the bluff that the night crew could use during the day. There was a rock ledge jutting out from the shore parallel to the sand that protected our swimming area a bit. It also was home to many tropical fish, coral, sea anemones, and bigger fish. Snorkeling around the ledge was like swimming in a tropical aquarium. One afternoon, PFC Tim

Howard speared a sizeable grouper with a homemade "Hawaiian Sling" spear. He took it up to the Mess Hall where they cooked it for him that night for dinner. On another afternoon he wanted to try to spear a small, 3-ft tiger shark, an interest I discouraged.

The path to beach was steep and uneven in its footing. So, on one afternoon PFC Howard and I carved out steps from the sun-baked clay and shored up the risers with planks of scrap wood[3].

Most nights were uneventful at the 91st Evac, but there was at least one memorable one. Dave Lynn and Elmo Vinas awoke one night with a knock on their hooch door. One of the Red Cross Donut Dollies asked them to help get a snake out of her second-floor room in the senior officers' quarters. As she was a little tipsy and had attended a party at the Special Forces compound that evening, Dave and Elmo wondered whether there was actually a snake in her room.

She explained when she opened her denim drawstring purse to get the key to her room, a snake popped out and slithered under her door into her room. When a skeptical Dave and Elmo turned on the light in her room, sure enough, a snake lay in the middle of the floor and quickly zipped under her metal wall locker.

Dave went back to his hooch to get a broom and a piece of 2x4. As Elmo pulled the locker away from the wall, Dave pinned the snake with the broom and bashed its head with the wood, Q.E.D.! This bit of commotion woke the surgeon in the next room, and being a curious guy, he took the dead snake the next morning to the Americal veterinarian to identify it. He learned it was a juvenile, multi-banded krait. Kraits are often referred to as a "two-step snake" as its lethal neurotoxin venom makes it one of the deadliest of all snakes. So much so, you'd be dead two steps after being bitten. The fact that the snake was immature didn't lessen the lethalness of its bite. We wondered if the snake had crawled into her purse at the outdoor party by itself or whether someone had put it in her bag as a practical joke?

While football played a role in M*A*S*H, volleyball figured in the 91st'EVAC's evenings in the officers' area. Our quality of play was a step up from 'picnic volleyball' but far from proper form. However, over time our discipline to use proper technique improved. A base camp-wide volleyball tournament helped us to do this.

We had entered our EM team in the competition, but the night of their first game our EM Club was having a rare floor show and our guys wanted to cancel being in the tournament. Dick Lamster, also our rec officer, asked if our officers wanted to play in their place? We did and eventually went on to win the tournament. When Special Services found out that we were a team of officers and not enlisted men, they did not want to award us the trophy.

I can't remember whether we received the trophy or not but a few months later a senior MSC general from Long Binh came visiting. When he learned we had won a volleyball tournament, he said to our CO, "We have a pretty good volleyball team in Long Binh. Maybe our team can play your team?"

Our CO agreed, and the general asked, "How much should we put on the outcome?"

Our CO shot back with, "How about $100?"

The game never took place, probably because there'd be too many officers having to travel to Long Binh or vice versa. Still, it was affirming that our CO would put up that much on our play. It wasn't a football game as in M*A*S*H, but the bets were made!

NOTES:

1. See L. Eisenbrandt (2015) <u>Vietnam Nurse, Mending & Remembering,</u> Deeds Publishing, Atlanta, GA, p.33.

2. One out of every ten Americans who served in Vietnam was a casualty. 58,148 were killed and 304,000 wounded out of 2.7 million who served. Although the percent that died is similar to other wars, amputations or crippling wounds were 300 percent higher than in World War II. 75,000 Vietnam veterans are severely disabled. https://www.google.com/search?q=number+of+us+-soldiers+wounded+in+vietnam&rlz=1C1CHZN_enUS915US915&o-q=number+of+wounded+in+Vietnam&aqs=chrome.1.69i57j0i22i-30j0i390.12733j1j15&sourceid=chrome&ie=UTF-8

3. When I returned to Chu Lai and the site for the 91st Evac, part of the cliff where the mess hall had been had fallen onto the beach. Our guide told us the local people called our little beach "Honeymoon Beach." It would be interesting to know why they named it that!

11. Mars-Venus Dilemma

It goes without saying, that the presence of females, Army nurses and Red Cross "Donut Dollies," at the 91st created a special environment, very different from the all-male units everywhere else in Vietnam. While in today's co-ed military, this may not seem so unique, but in the Vietnam War it was. It lent some everyday normalcy to our work environment but presented social challenges, especially for the women.

Some of the nurses and Red Cross women resented being 'hit on' by men they didn't know; others didn't mind being in a minority population. Those open to a romantic relationship had hard choices. First, Army protocol forbids nurses, who were officers, from fraternizing with enlisted men, most of whom were still single. On the other hand, many of the doctors and other officers their age were married. So, their dilemma was to break protocol or become "the other woman" for part of their tour. Second, did any man or woman want to be in a relationship in the fishbowl society of our compound? Especially for nurses and corpsmen who worked closely together, it presented a supervisor-subordinate red flag that is still an issue in any workplace today.

Some nurses had fiancés or husbands in nearby units. One of

our nurses was married to a warrant-officer pilot in a unit flying out of Chu Lai. Unfortunately, his helicopter crashed while skimming the S. China Sea. Apparently, his gunship unit was returning from a mission and thought it would be cool to see how low they could fly over the sea. All was great fun until he hit an 'air pocket' and dropped into the sea. Luckily, he survived and wound up recovering at the 91st.

The nurse I flew into Chu Lai with and who went on to the 27th Surg was engaged to a pilot who flew planes for the Air Force out of the Da Nang air base at Marble Mountain. He was a Forward Air Controller flying in a prop-driven, twin-tailed, fixed-winged airplane ahead of the bombing runs. His job was to mark enemy locations with flares for the bombers. Unfortunately, one day, his plane developed engine trouble in our area. While he was able to glide his craft enough to crash in the bay/cove at Chu Lai, he sustained a gash in his leg, and bled out before he could get to either nearby hospital. Many of us had seen or heard his plane sputtering and flying low over the main Chu Lai beach just before the crash. His death visibly pained the docs and nurses who knew the couple.

I saw the nurse again a few weeks later as she was getting together with some friends at the doctor's hooch who had the motorboat. I expressed my condolences for her loss. While she still seemed a little fragile, I sensed she was on the mend. Growing up it's one thing to mourn the death of an older relative, it's altogether another to lose a contemporary. For me that person was a high school classmate who died in an auto accident about two weeks before graduation. I still remember him to this day. I can't imagine the memories our veterans have who lost buddies in combat.

12. 91st Beach Rescue

When I tell most people that one of my jobs in Vietnam was "Beach Officer," they give me a quizzical look or assume that it must be duty a Marine officer in charge of a beach assault would have. Our little beach at the base of our bluff was one of the authorized sites for an official bathing beach in Chu Lai. The night crews and ambulatory patients enjoyed the respite that being on the beach in nice weather could bring. The curving cliffs that surrounded the beach and the rock reef made it a delightful place to sunbathe, swim, and snorkel during the dry season. On my first visit to the beach someone had a guitar, and a group of nurses and corpsmen were singing Pete Seeger's song *Where Have All the Flowers Gone* popularized by Peter, Paul, and Mary, among others. Their singing brought back memories of working at a summer camp and campfires in the Adirondacks during high school.

Americal Special Service facilitated getting the materials together to mark off our beach and the swimming area. They also provided the required rescue equipment. The only thing we didn't have was a high lifeguard tower/chair, but the beach was so small that one wasn't needed. To open our beach, the 91st Evac just had to provide the two qualified lifeguards. Special Services ran a week's training course at the main beach to train and approve guys to be lifeguards from all the approved beach units. I believe we sent about five guys down to the main beach for the training.

With all that cooperation and assistance, what could go wrong, right?! On Thursday morning of the certification training week, PFC Tim Howard came to me while I was looking in our Con-ex container for some spare parts. I said, "Hi, Tim; what are you doing, here? Aren't you supposed to be at the main beach getting tested?"

Tim replied, "Lieutenant Boyce, I only came to you to let you know I wouldn't be going down there today. I've had enough. Those water safety instructors at the Main Beach have been trying to drown us all week."

"But, Tim, we need you to get certified so we can reopen our beach," I replied.

Tim came back with, "Besides, I was the last guy from the 91st still going through the certification and we'd need at least two to pass to be able to open the beach."

"What do you mean, you're the ONLY GUY left in the course?" I asked. "Didn't we send about five guys down to take the training?"

Like a wise, old, beyond his years counselor Tim said, "Lieutenant Boyce, who do you think the wards were going to let go to take the lifeguard training? Most were the smack (heroin addicts) freaks. They all started to go through withdrawal once we got in the water for the physical training. As of yesterday, I was the only one left." He also let me know that today was the ¼-mile swim, which was well underway, and tomorrow was the three-rescue practical tests.

"Tell you what, Tim, how about if I go with you to take the tests to get certified?" I suggested. I was hoping that my Red Cross

Junior Lifesaving Course I had passed as a teenager in high school would be enough to pass the three-rescues practical test. "Please, go down or call the Main Beach to see if I can take the test with you tomorrow?" I pleaded.

Tim agreed and came back later saying, "Okay, they'll let us take the tests, tomorrow, BUT we'll have to do the ¼-mile swim after the 3-rescues." (There was a glimmer of hope!)

The next day, Tim and I presented ourselves with the remainder of the class for the three-rescues. We'd have to swim out three times to rescue our victim, a Water Safety Instructor who wasn't going to be a passive victim when we brought him to shore. I saw first-hand what Tim meant by them "trying to drown us." We had to rescue our victim first with a buoy, second with a surfboard and finally, with no flotation device to bring them in with a cross-chest carry. The first two rescues went smoothly as the victim had something stable to hold onto while I towed him in.

The fun started when I had to use a cross-chest carry to swim him into shore. Of course, about a few strokes toward shore, my victim "panics," slips my hold and grabs me around my neck to put my mouth and nose under water. Remembering how to parry a panicked victim, literally kicked in. I got a good breath and went below the surface and put my foot on his mid-section to push myself free. I reset the cross-chest carry, only tighter, and swam him to shore. My Junior Lifesaving training kicked in and things turned out smoothly.

After Tim and I finished with the 3-rescues, the head lifeguard pointed to the water and how far up the beach we had to go for our ¼-mile swim. It didn't really look that far; so, I dove in and started to do a relaxed Australian crawl headed up the beach line. After about five minutes of this, I looked to the beach and saw that I had made NO progress!! They had us swimming up-current! So, I had to switch to a stronger sidestroke to make any progress against the current and finally got to the end point, as did Tim.

My "drowning victim," a younger guy from California was nearing the end of his tour in Vietnam and contemplating signing up for a second year since he had a good gig at the Main Beach. (I'm sorry that I have forgotten his name.) Also, he felt that he had nothing to go back to since he had received a "Dear John" letter from his young wife asking for a divorce. While he was in a war zone, she couldn't get a divorce. I suggested that he should go back to the States for the remainder of his commitment; get the divorce, and get on with his life. That had to be better than spending another year in Vietnam.

Tim and I both passed and the beach at the 91st was good to go online the next day. Tim and I planned that he and I would call into the Main Beach first thing each morning to officially open. Since I really couldn't spend my days on our beach as a lifeguard, I figured I could be there to open it up, stay a half hour and then go up to the Motor Pool for my real work. The new NCO-in-Charge (NCOIC) of Special Services had an "ax to grind" with our unit and rightly figured that I wouldn't be on the beach all day. On the second or third day he came by in a motorboat later in the morning on a spot check. Finding only Tim on duty, he shut us down.

After about a week, two of the doctors on night shift came to complain to me that the beach was not open. I explained our situation for which they said, "Will they let us take the test and get certified?" I made a call to the Main Beach, and they agreed to test my volunteers. Both passed and we were allowed to reopen our beach with Tim and one of the two docs; a neurosurgeon and a thoracic surgeon, I believe. Their volunteering to fill the lifeguard staffing gap came as a relief. I was reminded, again, how people exist who are willing to contribute to the betterment of the unit. These docs could have remained on the sidelines and kept complaining about the beach being closed, but they stepped up to help. We need more of that today.

I ran into my "rescue victim" about two weeks later as he had come up to the hospital to have an nonhealing sore on his lip looked at. The doc told him it was probably due to sun damage, and he should have some of it cut away and sewn up to heal. He told me at that time, "Those two doctors you sent down to be tested performed the best of all those we've certified in Chu Lai!" The 91st had people with skills!

Night shift enjoying a sunny day on 91st beach.

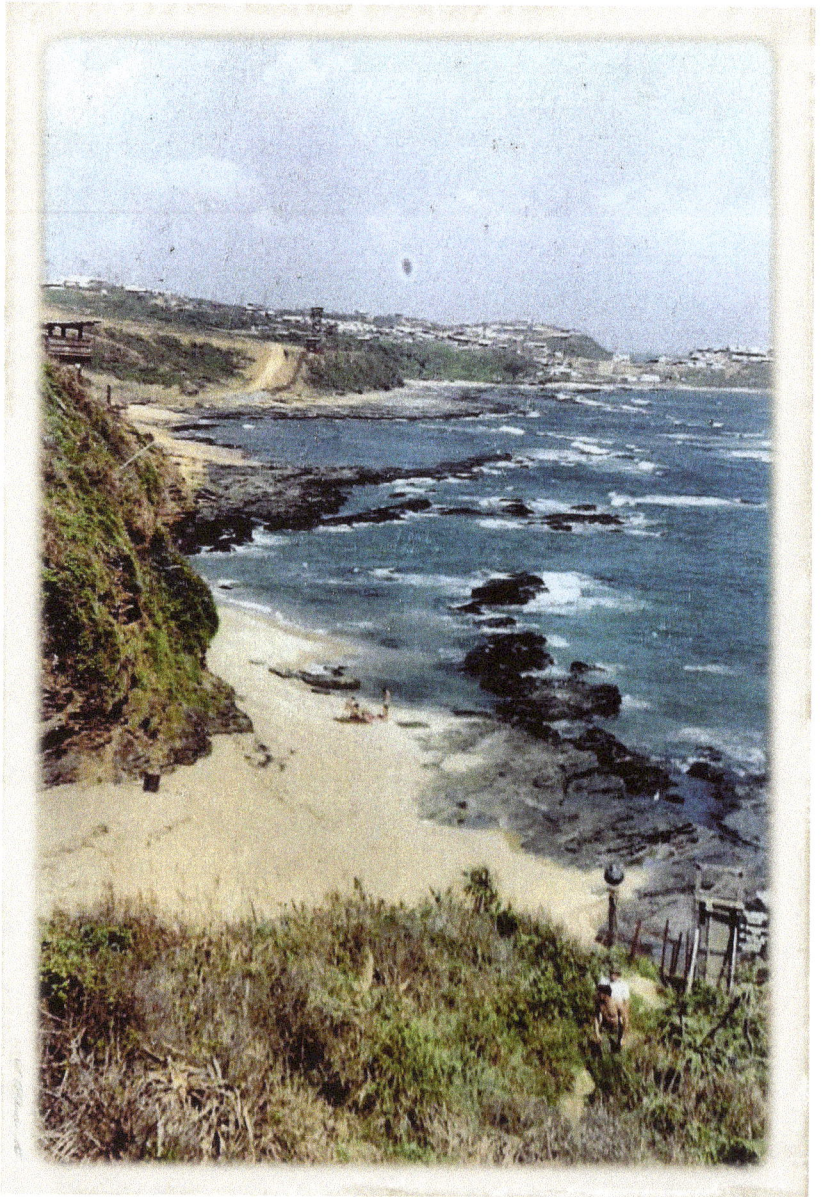

Looking down on 91st beach from O–Club.

13. Motorboat Martinet

The definition of a martinet is a strict but unwise or foolish disciplinarian, usually in the armed forces. They follow protocols to the letter, even when common sense would dictate otherwise. In more commonplace language, we would say that the new NCOIC of Special Services was a vindictive prick. This NCO had all the character of a *Nowhere Man* in the Beatles tune of the same name. I'd bet his lust for revenge led him to patrol our beach to find we only had one lifeguard on duty when two were required by the regs. That said, the low number of users on the beach on most days probably didn't really require two lifeguards. No, this NCOIC wanted something more: the doc's motorboat and his attempts to get it had been thwarted.

When the new NCOIC arrived in Chu Lai, he found that only one of the Main Beach's two motorboats was still operable and that his predecessor had hand-receipted/loaned out the other five motorboats to units in the base camp. It turned out that four of those five were now, also, inoperable, leaving the doc's motorboat as the only other boat that would run.

While I understand his reasoning for wanting it back, the way he went about trying to do so made him a superlative jerk. When he asked the doc who had it parked next to his hooch to return it, the doc refused as a group of docs and nurses enjoyed going out in the bay to waterski from time to time[1]. Whether their use constituted a 'greater good' won't be debated. It's what happened next which was inexcusable.

Having had his request refused, the NCOIC drove into the 91st Evac compound after midnight, hooked up the motorboat to his jeep and drove out, like an unauthorized repo man. In the morning, the docs reported the missing motorboat to our CO, who spoke with the American's commanding general, who, in turn, told the NCOIC to return the motorboat.

Did he? No way! The S.O.B. started the outboard motor and dropped it running into the water which sucked salt water into the air intake, seizing the pistons and rendering it inoperable! While I personally, "didn't have a dog in that fight," that NCOIC was certainly being a first-class, underhanded dirtbag. This account is a bit unusual for military in a war zone, as everyone works to support the mission and the politics and local fiefdoms of units on a post in the States are greatly reduced.

For this guy, I hoped the 'clerk mafia' would fix his wagon down the road. So, what is the clerk mafia? I learned of it when visiting American's finance office a month or two prior to returning to the States. The finance clerk related the following example. An NCO had been particularly overbearing to his clerk (usually a low-ranking GI with typing skills). The clerk called a friend in the unit's finance department who, without the NCO's knowledge, increased his net pay by about $50 a month. The NCO didn't report the discrepancy and enjoyed spending the extra funds. After about six months of these overpayments, the finance clerk informed the NCO that they had "discovered an error" and that they would claw back the funds in his next paycheck(s), leaving the NCO with no funds for a month or two. Bottomline to the story is that superiors should not mess over their clerks.

———————

NOTES:

1. For a picture of the motorboat, see Lou Eisenbrandt's book, <u>Vietnam Nurse Mending and Remembering</u>, Deeds Publishing, Athens, GA, (2015), p57.

14. Juicers, Potheads and Smack Freaks

1LT John Messina, an LSU graduate and devoted Archie Manning fan and an OCS-commissioned infantry officer in the Americal Division, had been out on patrols for a few months before coming to the 91st Evac for an eye exam. He wanted to get fitted for Army-issued glasses, the uncool, black plastic-frame kind. He had been wearing only his contacts and grew worried about having one pop out while he and his platoon were out on patrol. He wouldn't be able to read a topo map without his contacts. "It wasn't going to be wise for me to stop a patrol to look on the jungle floor for a lost contact, particularly at night," explained John.

After his eye exam, our optometrist asked, "How did you ever get into the Army because your eyesight is below induction standards?" (If only the character in *Alice's Restaurant* knew this?)

John asked, "Does this mean I can get discharged?"

"No, LT Messina, unfortunately, your eyesight is not below retention standards," replied our optometrist.

Because of his bad eyesight, John was given a "profile" that kept him out of field patrol assignments. Instead, around late fall/early winter 1970, he transferred in from the Americal Division to be our drug rehabilitation program officer. "What was this (unheard of) position?" we, MSCs, wanted to know. Up until this time the only Article 15 ("non-judicial punishment") discipline problems we really had in the 91st was arguments/fights between drunken EMs, a.k.a., juicers, and marijuana users, a.k.a., potheads in the barracks.

John related, "The Army has been "looking the other way" with marijuana use in Vietnam. Command didn't want punishments for marijuana use reflected on reports which might be made public. But now, they realize that 'smack' (heroin) use was becoming an issue." Generally, drug abuse was a rear-area issue as most soldiers wanted all their faculties out on patrols. If the soldier didn't care about that, his fellow patrol unit members probably did. We never got many details about John's work due to client confidentiality. Mainly, it was a troop education and getting detox help/counseling for those that asked for it. We started to see some of our own corpsmen at the 91st "nodding out," during duty hours or guys wearing their fatigue sleeves rolled down to hide their needle marks, despite the warm weather.

How did heroin use get started at the 91st? No one knew[1]. Some claimed that the pot was being laced with heroin and other substances to amplify the high. Possibly our guys got ahold of "OJ[2]" reefers? Our hospital laundry or some non-patient care duty became the workplace for many of our addicts. Still, their presence in the unit quickly led to a morale issue with our corpsmen, as the juicers and potheads would get Article 15 punishments for infractions viewed as minor compared to the smack freaks nodding out and not doing their jobs.

Upper command did not want to court martial and send addicts to Long Binh Jail (LBJ) in Saigon. They feared that more troops would intentionally become addicts to get out of combat duty. Despite trying to keep a lid on this situation, the military's heroin problem in Vietnam became a national public issue back home. Consequently, the Nixon administration instituted that all military returning from Vietnam must pass a urine test before they could board their flights back to the States. If you didn't pass, you went into a detox program before being permitted to fly home at the end of your tour.

Cynics in the military during the Draft years used to proclaim, "If they ran a business like the Army, it'd go bankrupt!" Unfortunately, I saw too many times in my business career where responsible managers delayed taking corrective action, waiting for the (politically) "right" decision to be evident. At least the military in the war zone placed a premium on leaders, who "do the right thing," over managers who "do things the right way." The marketing managers at the consumer products company where I first worked after my tour rarely gave the product development department definite guidelines with new product concepts. Consequently, a lot of resources were wasted generating any "new and improved" version. Sometimes shelving the work became the outcome. Eventually, the company sold our division and a few years later the whole company was bought out by another corporation.

One of the acknowledged benefits of a compulsory draft was that it brought in people who'd challenge some initial decisions, making for a better final decision and ultimate course of action. I just hope that with today's all-volunteer services that we still have more leaders over managers.

NOTES:

1. It was said that the heroin was being sold off the garbage truck that came into

our compound to collect the trash. It was run by local Vietnamese company approved for that job.

2.   Marijuana reefers where O stood for opium and J for Juana

Local Viet trash truck and suspected source of heroin.

Viet foreman of trash truck crew.

15. Mike Boat MedCap

It was another 8:00 a.m. MSC meeting with LTC Joe Gipson (whom we junior officers affectionately called, "The Hooter," after Hoot Gibson, an early cowboy film star). After all the usual administrative topics, LTC Gipson announced that he had secured the use of an Army "Mike boat" to take as many of the off-duty hospital staff that wanted to go on an Army Medcap[1] to an island offshore from Chu Lai.

At the 91st we'd send out a couple of doctors and nurses to visit the provincial hospitals near Chu Lai on unofficial Medcaps. It was a change of pace for our staff that went and, maybe, a benefit to the provincial hospital people they consulted with on these visits.

But this Medcap was different as anyone not on duty that day could go and only a handful of the medical team would treat the locals on the island. Meanwhile, the rest of us were free to swim and snorkel on the beach; and everyone would enjoy a cookout once the medical team had finished in the village.

This arrangement reflected LTC Gipson's out-going nature and personality of being a considerate leader with a host mentality. He valued keeping morale high and was always coming up with ideas, like this, to do that. Also, when senior brass was on site, he'd arrange some sort of entertainment for our guests and staff to enjoy and deepen working relationships.

But backup! What did he mean we'd take an ARMY "Mike boat?!" Who knew that the Army would have boats as equipment? Well, it did[2]. When we got to the dock, we saw a low, flat-bottom boat that could pass for a two-to-three car ferry boat back home. It easily held the 50, or so, staff that were making the trip. After getting on board, the Mike boat eased itself out from the dock and headed toward the horizon. It took a while before the island appeared on a sunny but hazy day. It promised to be a pleasant day in a war zone, evoking the mood of Otis Redding's *On the Dock of the Bay*.

The Mike boat anchored at the island's beach with its bow facing the sand and lowered the door-ramp for everyone to disembark. The medical team went to the village for sick call and the cooks set up the grills on the beach. The rest of us donned our bathing suits to enjoy the crystal-clear water. But we weren't the only ones in the water. A papa-san fisherman with a small, reed basket, a gaff hook, and a knife was diving and collecting sea urchins from the sandy bottom. He'd hook them and dump them in his basket, just like someone picking apples in an orchard. I watched him for a while, and he used his knife to hack open an urchin and scoop the insides into his mouth. I would never hear of sushi and sashimi for another 20 years; so little did I know he was eating some of the freshest sashimi anyone could wish for. My snorkeling mask let me see the many urchins on the seafloor at about 6-8 feet down. I had never seen urchins before but knew they were something you didn't want to step on.

Besides the sea urchins, there were large, midnight blue star fish: just beautiful! I had brought a Hawaiian sling spear in hopes of catching a fish to put on the grill with the hamburgers and hot dogs. Unfortunately, there was nothing big enough to spear. However, one of the docs from our nightly volleyball game swam over and wanted me to try to spear a sea snake he'd spotted. I declined as I knew that sea snake's venom was a neurotoxin and being a snake, it presented a very narrow target.

After a good swim, the medical team returned from the village and took a dip, the food was ready and we all enjoyed a good cookout of hamburgers, hot dogs, and the usual sides on the beach. Eventually, we reboarded the Mike boat and returned to Chu Lai as the sun was getting low.

NOTES:

1. Medcaps were supposed to be where medics in combat units/divisions held sick-call in local villages in an effort to "win the hearts and minds" of the population. These weren't normally an Army hospital program.

2. While designed as landing crafts, Mike boats (LCM-8, Landing Craft Mark-8), were used to transport freight and vehicles up the rivers in Vietnam

On board Mike boat heading out for MedCap.

Island for MedCap emerges on the horizon.

Island is another extinct volcano.

Staff not on MedCap enjoying beach.

16. The Mamas and Papas

In Vietnam, most GIs spoke hardly any Vietnamese and only a few locals spoke passable English. To be polite you'd address an adult male as "papa-san"; adult female as "mama-san" and young children as "boy-, girl- or baby-san." Supposedly, the suffix, "-san" is an east Asian honorific to show respect.

Every morning Vietnamese dayworkers, men and women, were admitted into Chu Lai base camp to do low-skill work, like housekeeping, warehouse maintenance, and mess hall help. In most cases, you never knew or were expected to know and correctly pronounce the names of our Vietnamese help. At the 91st our day help was overseen by Mister Biu (pronounced, "Boo"). He spoke English well and if you had an issue with your mama-san or papa-san, you spoke to him, and he'd take care of it.

A single mama-san would clean a couple of hooches and do the laundry of its residents. Our mama-san would put our dirty clothes into a plastic tub with soap and water and agitate them with her feet. After rinsing, the clothes would hang on a clothesline to dry. I can't say that Jim and I had a relationship with the woman looking after us due to the language barrier and to the fact she usually worked our hooch and laundry while we were at our jobs. Still, we appreciated her work.

Most of the mama-sans wore the straw cone hat, baggy black pants, and a light-colored, smock-like top. If it had been raining when they went to work that morning, they'd roll up their pant legs, but if a GI was nearby, they'd roll them back down out of modesty upon entering our compound.

One of the mama-sans that worked the senior doctors' and nurses' quarters seemed to be a "queen bee" to the others that worked the other officers' quarters. She had a modicum of English and displayed a good deal of grit and humor. She could give as well as take in a good-natured repartee. She would close out a debate with, "GI, YOU number one…HUNDRED THOUSAND!" I tried several times to take her picture, but she was very camera shy. I finally got a shot with a telephoto lens, but it doesn't do her justice.

The laundry hooch behind Jim's and mine came equipped with a washer and dryer and had covered clotheslines for the rainy season. The washer and dryer were for our female nurses' and Red Cross women's use. This arrangement wasn't a sign of male chauvinism as the nurses demanded the ability to do their own laundry. Apparently, the mama-sans took too much interest in seeing what American women wore under their uniforms. Some insight to the mama-sans' curiosity might be gained by reading the first few chapters of James Clavell's book, *Tai Pan*.

We had two papa-sans working in our Motor Pool. They'd take care of all the tire repairs. Woody built them an inflation protection cage by welding pieces of metal fencing stakes together with our acetylene torch. The cage was a safety measure as a metal ring on one side of the truck tire rim could pop out during inflation, posing an injury hazard for the person inflating the tire.

There were more papa-sans working in the warehouse and at the mess hall. The ones working in the warehouse cooked us a meal to celebrate Tet in 1971. I remember having colorful fried rice chips with some dipping sauce and a rice and chicken gruel. Any other items on the menu have evaporated from my memory.

Early in my tour, Dave Lynn and I had just captured a big, gray moth with brown spots on its wings in his office. We had killed it with a solvent and left it on his desktop to dry. We had intentions of mounting it to show to our colleagues. Just then, a papa-san cleaning the admin hooch came into Dave's office, so we stepped out in the hall to continue our conversation. The papa-san seemed to be taking a little more time than usual in his floor sweeping chore, so we peeked in … just as he deftly scooped up the big moth and popped it in his mouth!

Late in my tour at the 91st I was given the project to replace our perimeter barbed wire fence. I had a crew of a few corpsmen, guys with known drug problems, and some papa-san day workers. Replacing the fence on the south side of our compound went reasonably smooth. The only issue was pounding the metal fence stakes into the hard clay soil between the 91st and the transportation unit abutting us. The issue was whether the guy wielding he sledgehammer could reliably hit the top of the metal stake and not hit the guy holding it before the stake would remain upright on its own. A spent artillery shell placed on top of the stake presented a better target for the guy wielding the sledgehammer. Even then, it took a good effort to get the stake into the ground. It was hot, physical work as depicted in Sam Cooke's 1960 song, *Chain Gang*.

The perimeter section between the 91st and the amphitheater bowl for the Bob Hope shows presented an additional challenge: foliage. In the 50 feet or so between the Quonset hut wards and the fence, shrubs and vines had grown and had to be removed. While working this section I noticed some of the papa-sans seemed to be intrigued with some of the vines on the old fence. I finally went over to see what they were up to and saw them plucking orange spheres from the vines. These orange-colored berries, as big as a boy's marble, were inside a papery shell, resembling a Chinese paper lantern. One of the papa-sans offered me one, which I ate more out of politeness; but to my pleasant surprise, it had a flavor like honeydew melon.

We sprayed diesel fuel on the brush to defoliate it as Agent Orange usage had stopped. While diesel fuel did the job, it took a couple of hours for the leaves to dry out. As the wait slowed our progress considerably, I decided to have our guys spray a little more diesel on the plants so we could light it and let fire do the work. The first trials worked well; so emboldened, I had the crew spray a larger area before we set fire to it. Unfortunately, this section had larger bushes and came closer to the hospital Quonset huts. The resulting flames rose so much that I had the orderly room call for the Americal fire team. Luckily, the flames had died down considerably by the time the fire fighters arrived, no hospital areas were damaged, but I felt embarrassed for my impatience. Lesson learned that day!

During my tour, most of our local help impressed me with their work ethic. Most locals in our area were farmers and, like those in the States, worked hard and were adept at improvising to get the job done. In the early 1970's their water buffaloes supplied their tractor power in the rice fields and bicycles, moped, and Lambretta mini-trucks got them from place to place.

NOTES:

1. In pidgin English, "number one" was good; and "number ten" was bad.

Our mama-san who cleaned our hooch and did our laundry.

A moth like the one the papa-san ate

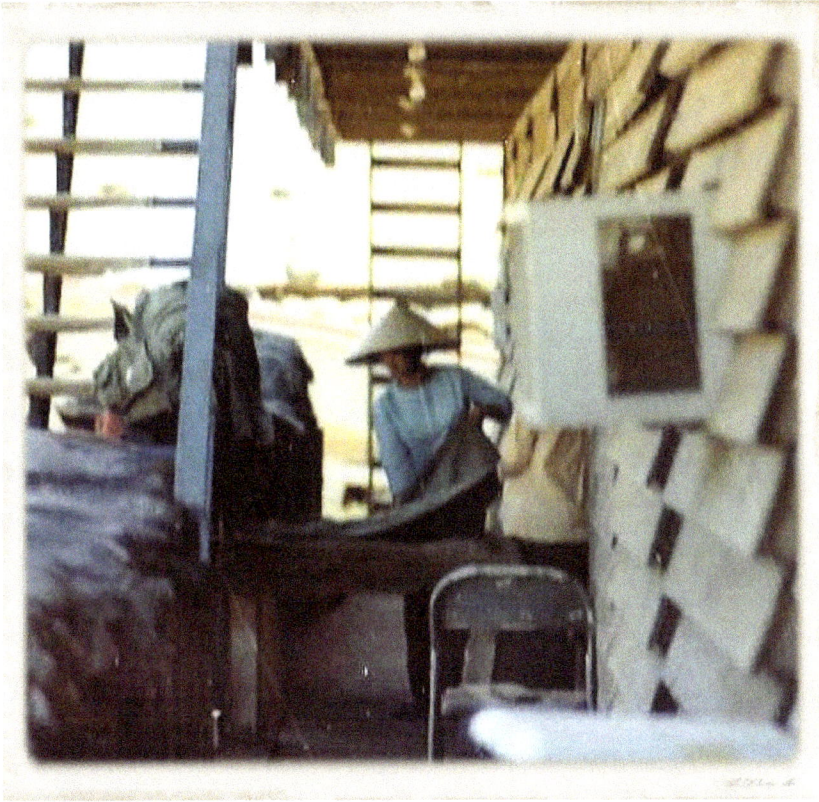

The spunky mama-san ironing by the senior officers' and nurses' quarters

Our two hardworking papa-sans in the motor pool.

17. Escorting USO Visits

Besides sending bands to play at EM- and Officer Clubs in the base camps and sometimes the fire bases, the USO would send groups of celebrities to visit the patients in our hospital. The sick and the wounded GIs appreciated the visits from pro sports figures. I don't know how I got picked to escort two of these groups, but I learned a lot from them ... as much as they learned from their visits.

The first tour consisted of several Major League Baseball players. Before entering a ward, I had to prepare them for the kind of patient they'd meet. For the surgical wards, I let them know that they'd see some severely wounded men: amputees and shrapnel wounds. I counselled them not to react to the severity of what they saw but to engage each patient calmly in conversation if the patient was up for it.

I had never met pro baseball players before and didn't know what to expect. I was proud that one was a Baltimore Oriole which is the baseball team I had gone to watch as a kid in Maryland. I was impressed with how this group handled their visit to the wards. They seemed to have a counselor's touch in their approach. The patients really seemed to brighten up when they'd stop by their beds. These guys really tried to make the patient's life a little better, in the spirit of the Beatles song in *Hey Jude*.

A few months later I was asked to escort a group of NFL players. They were a larger, more boisterous group, typical jocks you'd meet on any college campus. I gave the same orientation about the severely wounded before we entered the surgical wards. However, I had an extra warning to give before we entered the medical ward.

Medical wards in an Evac Hospital have those being treated for conditions such as diseases, dysentery, chronic sores, and antibiotic-resistant VD. The day the NFLers visited we had a hepatitis patient on the medical ward. Unlike all the other patients, they were not to shake this patient's hand, as hepatitis is highly transmissible. I informed them that there was a sign on the wall by the patient's bed stating, "hepatitis." So, I advised them to maintain their distance when visiting with this patient.

I think we must have been on the ward not more than about five minutes when I noticed an offensive end from the Atlanta Falcons (I'll call him, Larry) shaking hands with the hepatitis patient. When he stepped away to go to another patient, I pulled him aside and said, "Larry, that was the patient you were not supposed to shake hands with."

A bit worried he said, "What's going to happen now? Am I going to get it?"

I then told him what a nurse had told me on what to do in this situation, "Go over to that table and wash your hands in that brown solution in that bowl." It was filled with betadine, a strong disinfectant.

Larry said, "That's ALL I have to do? Wash my hands in that solution and I'll be fine?"

"Yes," I answered.

Next thing I know, Larry calls one of his tour-mates over to meet the hepatitis patient and shake his hand. After doing so, he points out the hepatitis sign on the wall by the patient. His buddy blanches and then Larry laughs and shows his buddy the bowl of betadine to disinfect his hands! What some people will do for a joke. Needless to say, the ward nurse that afternoon was not amused.

Still, I appreciated these sports pros taking time to travel to the Vietnam war zone on their own time to give back to the wounded GIs. They brightened the patients' day, maybe giving hope to some of getting through their healing and rehab processes. Happily, the USO continues to bring celebrities to our troops stationed around the world.

18. Notable Casualties

The evacuation time from the battlefield to our ER was very fast, said to be no more than about 30 minutes. This meant that more wounded soldiers survived with lifelong disabilities whereas they would have probably died enroute to a doctor in an ambulance during WWII and the Korean Conflict[1].

The Vietnam War distinguished itself from the WWII and Korean wars in that there was a 300% increase in the number of severely disabled casualties due to boobytraps, what we now call IEDs[2]. The Americal Division operated in an area where Ho Chi Minh got the Viet Minh together to overthrow the French, so their area of operation contained a large population of Viet Cong-allied people. While a small-unit patrol in other areas in Vietnam might encounter two boobytraps in a year, those in the Americal might encounter two in a day[3].

One of the criticisms of Michael Cimino's film, *The Deer Hunter*, is the showing of Russian Roulette as something the Vietnamese played and wagered on. Personally, I believe it is an apt metaphor of what it must have been like for the Americal infantryman's experience out on patrol. Since there were command-detonated traps as well as trip-wired triggered one, no manner of self-preparation, position in the patrol, or alertness could increase your chances of survival in the field. The constant stress of being killed or severely wounded on patrol, in my mind, approaches that of playing Russian Roulette.

Once when Jim, my hooch-mate, went to the ER on rotation, four burn victims arrived. They were burned over more than 60% of their body area, which meant that they had a low chance of survival. They were the crew of a 5-ton tanker truck carrying a load of fuel up Highway 1. The VC had recovered a dud 500-lb bomb our jets had dropped somewhere else. They buried it under the road and command-detonated it when the tanker drove over it. The guy who was burned the most had initially been blown clear of the flames but went back to try to drag his buddies out.

Jim said the burns on their torsos contracted the skin, restricting their breathing. To relieve the constriction, the docs cut a slit down the middle of their chests to ease their breathing. They were given morphine for their pain and the burns dressed as well as they could. These guys survived long enough to be put on a plane to the hospital at Yokohama, Japan. Some or all may have expired on that trip or in Japan. If they didn't, their next stop would have been Brooke Army Hospital at Ft Sam, which had the best burn unit in the US at the time.

Another notable casualty during my tour was a quadruple amputee. One night around midnight when I was the Officer of the Guard, I met a rabbi chaplain coming down the hospital boardwalk. As an outsider on-site after curfew, I stopped him to learn what brought him in at that time of day. He had been visiting a Jewish soldier who had stepped on a boobytrap while out on patrol. The blast took both legs and injured both arms so badly that the surgeons had to amputate them too. What was unusual for this soldier's injuries is that no shrapnel fragments hit any of his vital organs. Still, with these injuries at this early stage, his survival was questionable. However, this guy recovered enough to be evacuated on to Japan and the States.

I had always wondered what happened to him. I found out during the 1972 Presidential election. CBS News ran a story about a quadriplegic vet who wrote a letter to President Nixon that never got a reply. The footage showed him at a typewriter using a pencil in his mouth to push the keys to write his letter. The CBS story told us that, before he was drafted, this GI had been the president of his college campus "Students for Nixon" political group for the 1968 election. In his letter to Nixon in 1972, he expressed his disappointment that Nixon had not kept his campaign promise to get the US out of Vietnam, so he'd never have had to go to war. This guy really embodied the spirit in Jerry Butler's 1968 song, *Only the Strong Survive.*

Besides combat casualties, there were plenty of non-combat casualties. One of the most common that killed or hurt GIs in the rear were M151 jeep rollovers. Unlike the jeeps in WWII, these Ford jeeps had a narrower wheelbase that made them tippy in turns, even at low speeds.

As I mentioned about the beaches in Chu Lai, there were drownings. We lost a corpsman, Danny, who with a couple of buddies went down to the rocks below our bluff to smoke a reefer or to shoot up heroin. They decided to do this on a Jan/Feb afternoon during our monsoon season when the winds whipped up the waves in the Chu Lai cove. The angry grey surf hardly made it a day anyone would want to go to the beach! The guys selected a spot where their activities could not be observed but this location involved hopping over a vee-gap in the rocks above the surf. Only problem was that when waves hit the vee-gap and then the cliff wall, the wave would rebound and shoot up a water spike when it met another incoming wave.

One of these water spikes grabbed Danny when he went to jump on the way back. He fell into the vee-gap and was knocked unconscious by the pounding waves. How his buddies got him out and on shore, I don't know. I do remember trying to revive him with chest compressions and mouth to mouth resuscitation, only to get unresponsive gurgles. His buddies had gotten him out too late.

Another non-combat death would have earned a Darwin Award had they been around at that time. One afternoon a jeep came racing into our compound and didn't stop at our guard shack to register. The driver pulled up at hospital ramp between the Hospital Orderly Room and Dental Clinic yelling for a corpsman and a gurney. His buddy in the jeep, had a head wound.

The injured soldier was a "short timer" meaning he had a month or two before he'd go back to the States. Short timers looked down on the FNGs (F*ing New Guy) in their units. (Because replacements came in one or two at a time to units, everyone else in your unit had fewer days than you[4].) Upon meeting someone with less time left before DEROSing, the FNG would hear the verbal dig, "…if I had that much time left, I'd shoot myself!"

Apparently, the injured guy had been playing cards with a bunch of guys, one a newbie. The guy picked up a .45 revolver, put it to his head and pulled the trigger, thinking it was empty when he said, "If I had that much time left, I'd shoot myself." He didn't survive.

Besides wounded American soldiers our hospital treated enemy combatants, NVA and VC, and local civilians. Our medical staff would do their best to treat the Vietnamese wounded, no matter what their allegiance. Once healed, the VC wounded would be sent to "Chu Hoi"/reeducation camps run by the South Vietnamese government. The NVA wounded would transfer to a government POW camp for interrogation. The docs weren't happy about treating enemy casualties, but they were faithful to their Hippocratic Oath.

For local civilian casualties, it was not uncommon for their family members to come to be with them on the Vietnamese ward. Below is a picture of one of our nurses caring for a Montagnard baby whose mother was injured and on the ward that day.

NOTES:

1. J. Aaron & K. Miller (September 20200) "Vietnam War: Medical Treatment and Training" DoD Legacy Program Report, Washington, DC, p.2-9.

2. S. Neel (1991) <u>Medical Support of the US Army in Vietnam 1965-1971</u>, Dept of the Army, Washington DC, p.173

3. Americal G-2 Briefing to 91st Evac officers, Spring 1971.

4. One of the improvements we see in the deployment of troops to war zones is that whole units go over and DEROS together. I think this must instill a team like working environment. Also, it seems that the tours of duty in the war zone are shorter: ~6 months vs 12 months as was in Vietnam.

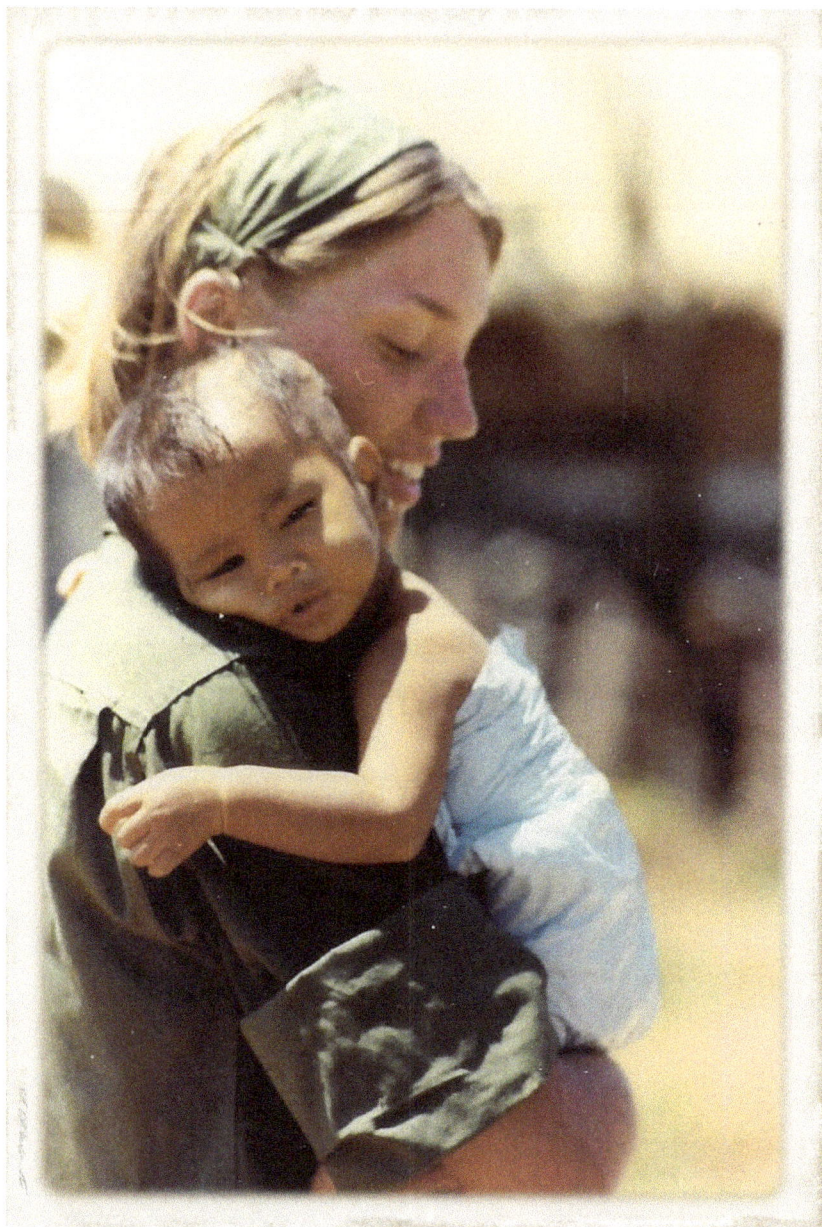

91st nurse caring for Montagnard baby while mother was in surgery.

19. Motor Pool "Going Junking"

Becoming the hospital's Motor Officer was a challenge from the get-go. While I had a cursory interest in automobile mechanics, and could perform the basic operator maintenance tasks, like changing the oil, changing spark plugs and keeping tires inflated to the proper pressure, I now inherited responsibility for several diesel trucks as well as a jeep and two ¾-ton, gasoline-fueled utility trucks. I knew that I'd have to rely heavily on the technical advice of my motor sergeant.

I may have been the first Motor Officer as the Motor Pool reported to our Supply Officer and, previously, he had left the day-to-day running of the Motor Pool to its Motor Sergeant. Within a month of getting this job, the 91st had an I.G. inspection which included the Motor Pool. Apparently, we had not done well and LTC Gipson said that I wouldn't be held responsible for the low scores in our area.

Luckily, my new Motor Sergeant, SGT Charles Woods, a.k.a. Woody, arrived at the time I took over. He had worked in garages in civilian life and knew his way around a shop. Together we emphasized basic Operator Maintenance for the trucks. Previously, when a driver from the warehouse wanted a truck, he'd sign out whatever truck was available in the Motor Pool.

Woody suggested we'd assign each deuce-and-a-half to a specific driver from the Warehouse. In this way, the drivers took ownership of their vehicles and had a vested interest in keeping up the Operator Maintenance duties. These duties included draining water from the diesel fuel filters, keeping the tires inflated to the proper pressure, changing the oil, and lubing the ball joints in the undercarriage. This left Woody, PFC John Rink, and CPL Capps to work on the more important jobs, like brakes, wheel bearing lubrication and/or replacements, alignments, tune-ups, and minor component replacements. Specialized vehicle maintenance units in Chu Lai carried out the more complicated jobs, like engine or transmission rebuilds. However, we never had the need to send any of our trucks up for that kind of work.

That said, we did do one job beyond our authorization. I don't know how he did it, but Woody got a hold of a brand, new six-cylinder motor, originally meant for a gasoline powered forklift. He said that it would fit one of our ¾-ton utility trucks and we had one that was running badly. I had friends in high school who talked about switching out motors of a Pontiac or Chevy, but I had never seen it done. I can't remember how Woody and Rink were able to get the old motor out and the new one in. Possibly, they got assistance from PFC Radmer, driver of the big forklift at the warehouse. He could have looped a chain around its forks and raised it out. Otherwise, we may have had a winch in the Butler building bay.

I don't think there were any serious complications that weren't overcome. If there was an issue, it could have been with the union between the motor's flywheel and the transmission's clutch, sort of what Johnny Cash sung about in his 1976 song about smuggling out Cadillac car parts out of an assembly plant in *One Piece at a Time*. Nevertheless, the job was successful, and the utility truck hummed with its new given life. We all got an extra bounce in our step that afternoon

Unfortunately, within a month or two, the new motor was ruined! A driver took the truck out for an errand. As he was a heroin addict, this time he took it out of our compound to get high. He nodded out while parked with the engine running. What do idling car engines do in the summertime? They overheat. When the driver came to, the engine was red hot with steam pouring out. The excessive heat warped the piston rings so now the new engine ran like the old engine. I felt so sorry for Woody and Rink after all their good work on this job, but they took it well as best they could.

Getting replacement parts for our trucks was not that easy. Our replacement parts came from an Americal supply depot about a mile away in Chu Lai. Too many times our part would be on back order. Once Woody and I drove up to check on how soon a hydraulic brake system part, called a hydrovac, would be in. Hydrovacs were a common failure and always on back order according to the lieutenant that ran the supply depot. He was apologetic and explained that their system was down at that moment; so, he couldn't get an update on when the order would likely come in. Why? There had been a power outage in their area the day before and his computer went down. The mainframe-type computer ran on punch cards, and it would take at least a day for his clerks to feed the cards back into it to reprogram their inventory.

With that bad news, Woody showed me his "Plan B." He introduced me to "going junking." On the way to the supply depot, we passed an area where numerous wrecked vehicles sat in overgrown vegetation. While many had been relieved of their hydrovacs, we were lucky to find one after a few tries. The vegetation around the trucks presented an additional caution: watch out for snakes! The life lesson learned that day was to always have a Plan B, a contingency, should your initial course of action prove impossible. Unfortunately, this resource became off-limits a month or two later because the wrecked trucks had been sold! Huh?? We never found out who exactly bought them, why or what they did with them?

Returning to the motor pool, Woody with a smile and a chuckle promised to "make a shade-tree mechanic" out of me yet. He showed me how to lube the undercarriage of a deuce-and-a-half and how to rebuild brake cylinders and to bleed brakes when replacing shoes in our grease pit. This prepared me to knowledgeably inspect our trucks from time to time. I did a brake job on my own car once I got home before cars got too sophisticated for amateurs to work on.

Officially, CPL Capps was our PLL clerk in charge of keeping our replacement parts in stock. PLL stands for Prescribed Load List, a list of parts a unit was authorized to have on hand. We had a room with cabinets to hold these parts, but the ones we had on hand were mostly the ones we rarely needed. Capps would place orders with the supply depot for the frequently replaced parts, like brake shoes, and we'd receive them in a day or two. Unfortunately, some parts, like a hydrovac, were hard to get. A truck would have to sit idle, "red-lined," when critical parts were on back order.

An acetylene torch was another piece of equipment we weren't supposed to have in our unit. Its hoses had seen better days as evidenced by the numerous places where black tape patched old leaks. Our torch only had a cutting tip, so welding the frame for our tire inflation safety cage took some skill and a lot of brazing rods.

One afternoon I was over at the grease pit when I heard shouting and looked over to the Butler building bay to see Rink and Alfie Mailott running as fast as they could out the doors. Then, there was a sharp explosion and very dense, black smoke came shooting out the doors over their heads. Either the hoses to the acetylene torch developed a new leak or a patch failed, and the hose blew up. While we still had the tanks and the torch, we had to find some way to get new hose, and a welding tip, if we wanted to use it again.

In Vietnam, there was no saluting of officers as this was a security risk, especially in the field. Uniform neatness was way laxed, even in the rear, as long as the work got done. From time to time, I tried to cajole my guys to put a little effort in their appearance by telling them, "You're not really in Vietnam (where conditions are relaxed). You're actually at a secret Army installation outside Ft. Huachuca[1] in Arizona." I'd get a laugh and the usual retort of, "What are you going to do (if I don't), send me to Vietnam?"

Before we knew it, most of our year was getting near its end and our second IG inspection in the Motor Pool came unannounced. While I had spent some time in the PLL shack over the preceding months after CPL Capps DEROSed, getting the records up to date was always a losing battle. Still, it was better than when I took over. Woody and I did wonder whether we'd get dinged for some of the truck paint jobs not being the official OD-green.

After the IG team left, Woody came up with a solemn and serious look on his face to tell me what they had told him. He broke into a Cheshire Cat grin and said, "They said these were probably the best maintained trucks they'd seen in Vietnam." Kudos to Woody and Rink!

NOTES:

1. Ft. Huachuca is in a remote area of Arizona near the Mexican border. It had the reputation of being a fun-less place to be stationed. A quote from Wikipedia on Ft. Huachuca: "The area is so desolate and barren that an old army

description of the fort states, "It is the only fort in the Continental United States where you can be AWOL for three days and they can still see you leaving."

Butler building housing motor pool bay on the left and warehouses.

PFC Rink's dump truck.

PFC Radmer driving unauthorized forklift donated by departing Seabees with SGT Woods aboard.

20. A Night at DOOM

The accommodations for the Army in a war zone pale in comparison to what the Navy and Air Force enjoy. I became aware of this on one of my trips to Da Nang to visit MAJ Pedersen to work on revising the TO&E. While I had been impressed with the Officers' Mess Hall that the Navy ran, I was blown away by the Da Nang Officers' Open Mess (DOOM), the Air Force's O-club at their air base. My point in this account is that there's a difference between which branch of service a REMF is in. In this regard, the Army might be considered the "red-headed stepchild" versus its sister services.

Our O-club at the 91st was a wood-sided, tin-roofed frame building with plexiglass windows fogged a bit due to the sun. It was probably as big as a double-wide, manufactured home. The American Division's O-club, though larger, served pizza made from sauce, hot dog slices, and cheddar cheese (Ugh!). On the other hand, the DOOM was masonry and spacious. On entering, I saw a TV behind the bar, playing a delayed broadcast of the Mohammad Ali-Oscar Bonavena fight, which Ali won. Inside, one could easily envision he was in a V.F.W. club stateside.

I was able to get a steak dinner, something missing on our mess hall's menu. That evening an American band played for their floor show. At the 91st our EM-and O-clubs usually got Korean or Filipino bands. While they played well, they didn't' remind you so much of home. So, a band from the States was a treat.

The band played well, in my humble opinion. Nearing the end of the set, the lead singer, a pretty, young, woman was singing *Age of Aquarius/Let the Sunshine In*, which many bands included in their sets to open or close a show. As she was putting her heart and soul into her song, my peripheral vision caught something white flying in the air from behind me toward the stage. At first, I thought nothing of it, but then, more pieces of white stuff flying followed, some landing on the stage.

When I turned around, I saw that the white stuff was pieces of bread emanating from a table of four senior Air Force officers: majors, and a lieutenant colonel. They were dressed in very colorful jump suits, black, red, cerulean blue, and bright yellow. These "drinking suits" were heavily embroidered with images of dragons and maps of Vietnam. I don't know if the guy tearing pieces of bread was targeting the band on the stage or just one of his fellow pilots at his table. That is, were the pieces that landed near the stage intentional or just "collateral damage?" It didn't matter to the musicians: they abruptly left the stage. The fight escalated when one of the combatants picked up a seltzer bottle to squirt his fellows, which is when I departed!

While I appreciate that the services with the cargo planes and vessels can easily bring in extras that Army and Marine units in-country normally will lack, I didn't understand this departure from reasonable, courteous behavior.

21. Home Leave and Hong Kong R&R

A couple of months after I had arrived in-country, the Army announced that service members with accrued leave could take two-weeks of it in a return trip to the US. Otherwise, breaks from the war zone would be in approved R&R locations: Bangkok, Taipei, Hong Kong, Sidney, or Honolulu.

Home leave was appealing as it was less expensive than meeting Jean in an R&R location and I could have a chance of seeing the rest of our families. I took it at the half-way point in my tour which put me home just after Christmas. I don't remember many specifics about that leave other than it was cold with snow-covered ground. I know I spent time with Jean at her folks' place in New Jersey and my parent's farm in Maryland.

I got to watch that year's Bob Hope show at my grandmother's house on her color TV rather than in Vietnam. I don't remember where that show was filmed in 1970, only that it wasn't in Chu Lai due to security concerns in our area of operations. The amphitheater in Chu Lai hosted the shows in 1967, 1968 and 1969.[1]

The big drag with home leave in the US was having to go back to Vietnam! My first six month seemed to take an eternity and the prospect of another interminable wait really bummed me out. The only plus on my trips to/from the US this time was that my planes took the polar route through Yokohama, Japan, and Anchorage, Alaska. This route meant only 18 hours point-to-point, rather than the 27 hours it took on my initial flight to Vietnam.

In late spring 1971, I still had an R&R trip coming to me. So, I decided to take advantage of R&R in one of the Asian locations: Bangkok, Taipei, and Hong Kong. Honolulu and Sidney just seemed too far to travel, and I felt these locales would exacerbate my wanting to be back home. "So close, yet still far away," so to speak.

I chose Hong Kong and Jim Robbins, my hooch mate, was going there too. Arriving at Hong Kong's now "old" airport was exciting as our landing path went low over the roof tops of apartment buildings under the landing pattern. We were so low in our approach that if our windows could open, you could probably grab some drying laundry before we touched down.

A permanent party military guy gave us a "dos and don'ts" orientation on our way into town to our hotels, which were mostly in Kowloon, rather than downtown Hong Kong on Victoria Island. One important watchout was to look a different way when crossing streets as traffic ran on the opposite side of road, as in Britain. It took a couple of days and a few close calls to get used to this change.

The hustle and bustle of this city was a big change from Chu Lai. People of all ages were going about their daily lives, unconcerned with warfare. Hong Kong and Kowloon was in a building boom with the erection of many skyscrapers. The scaffolding around these projects, composed of bamboo lashed together impressed me greatly. Construction workers scurried up them as our workers in the US would on metal scaffoldings.

Being low on funds because most of my pay went home to Jean

and Lee, I knew I wasn't going to be spending a lot at the PACEx store in Hong Kong. Most soldiers loaded up at PACEx on stereo equipment, SLR cameras, Seiko watches, and jewelry. Also, I wasn't going to be buying tailor-made suits, like the guys with fatter wallets.

So, I offered to be a purchasing agent for anyone who wanted me to pick up something while I was there. A male nurse asked if I'd pick up an "dark green, imperial jade wedding band with gold edges" for his wife. At the jewelry counter inside PACEx, the salesgirl educated me on the foolishness of this request.

"First, due to its high cost and the waste generated in making a wedding band, no one would want to make a ring out of imperial jade. You might get one made from Burmese soapstone, which looks like jade but is much cheaper," she informed. She showed me some brooches made from imperial jade, some of which were white with green veining. Also, she showed me some pieces of carved Burmese soapstone, which was the green color one usually associates with jade but lacked the translucent quality in imperial jade.

Interestingly, later that day I passed a street vendor hawking what my client had asked for: jade colored wedding band lined with gold-toned metal. He wanted a reasonable price for his piece, IF it was imperial jade. It was clear that it wasn't, so I declined to buy. He immediately dropped his price and we dickered for a few minutes. I was not happy with the metal work surrounding the green stone band. I finally declined and started to walk away at which he offered, "Six Hong Kong dollars," which was equal to one US dollar. I thought about accepting but I was afraid the gold-toned metal surrounding the band might turn my friend's wife's finger green if he gave it to her.

GIs on R&R in Hong Kong stood out like sore thumbs because

of our taller physical builds and our "white wall" haircuts. No sooner did Jim and I step into the street from our Army-approved R&R hotel in Kowloon, we were swarmed with guys recommending tailor shops where we could get suits and shirts made at a good price. We declined as we weren't in the market for these wares and heard stories that sometimes the stitching came apart after getting back home and that while a good fit when made, they'd become too tight after we put on weight after returning home.

I first learned to eat a meal with chopsticks in Hong Kong. When Jim and I asked about a restaurant recommendation our first night, our hotel concierge said, "The Glass Slipper." I had seen it mentioned in a tourist brochure as a restaurant catering to westerners with a floor show. Due to my budget, I asked the concierge, "Where do you go for a meal around here?" He said, "The Purple Orchid across the street." I thanked him and that's where we had our first meal without forks.

When we sat down at our table and asked for forks, our waiter informed us that they didn't have them. I think we may have been the only westerners in there that evening. Our waiter kindly showed us how to use them and we did our best to copy his technique. While we succeeded in getting food into our mouths and not down the front of our shirts, it was challenging. Soon, our hands started to cramp, which lessened in later meals as we became more facile with chopsticks. Being open to trying new ways of doing things may not always be easy but one gains insight in what's it like to "walk in another's shoes." Today, when my wife and I eat in an Asian restaurant, I always ask for the chopsticks.

After a couple of meals of Cantonese, we wanted a change. I saw in one of the tourist magazines that there was an Indonesian restaurant, not too far away, offering "rijsttafel" which Jean and I had enjoyed in Amsterdam on our honeymoon. This dish is really a big bowl of rice served with several smaller bowls containing savory meats and/or vegetables in sauces. You put rice on your plate and add something from one of the small dishes. Then you can try another small dish in the same manner.

We were working our way through the six or seven bowls of tasty preparations until we came to one that looked like noodles in a peanut sauce. Although when I picked up some noodles with my chopsticks and put them into my mouth, their shape seemed plumper than spaghetti and both ends of the noodles came to a point. Once I took a bite, I knew I wasn't eating a pasta! I looked at Jim and asked him, "Any idea of what this could be?"

Jim's expansive reply, "Could be Ascaris."

"What's that?" I asked.

Referring to an operation we witnessed in the 91st OR, Jim elaborated, "Do you remember those round worms that the surgeon took out of that baby-san's intestine? I'll bet these are probably sea worms[2]." With that comment, I stopped chewing and gagged down what was in the back of my mouth.

Jim had reminded me of two laparotomy surgeries at the 91st. The first was the resection of perforated intestines of a soldier. The second was a young girl who had similar wounds that needed to have a section of intestine removed and bleeding blood vessels cauterized. However, when the surgeon cut open her intestine, he pulled out several 8"-10" round worms and put them in a bottle for disposal before he could finish his work. Those worms had a strong resemblance to whatever it was in the peanut sauce. It's nice to try things from other cultures, but this dish was a stopping point for me. Later in life, I worked with colleagues who traveled to China for work with our subsidiary. They often had similar encounters with foods we don't usually eat. Some learned deft ways of deferring the honor of the special treat to someone else.

One tourist offer we did opt for was a package of three tours of the area: Victoria Island, Hong Kong at Night, and the New Territories. Our very pretty Chinese tour guide led us on all three. On the Victoria Island tour, which at the time was the old city and business center, we saw Tiger Balm Gardens[3], and Repulse Bay, a place where locals could enjoy an afternoon at the beach. We made a stop at the Aberdeen fishing village at the beach where the fishermen dried their catch…an unbelievably pungent and unpleasant aroma. I couldn't imagine what it'd be like working as a fisherman on that beach.

The Hong Kong at night tour treated us to a wonderful meal in a floating restaurant and took us to the Tai Pak[4] amusement park to see a traditional Chinese drama/opera where the performers wore elaborate masks and moved at the beat of drums and gongs. Obviously, we didn't understand a word, but our guide said that the performers used an old version of Chinese that she did not fully understand either.

On our tour of the New Territories, we got out of the city proper to more scenic areas and smaller cities. One, we were told, was the "town of the people who eat dogs." Our guide remarked that we wouldn't find strays in this town. We stopped for a bio-break and snack at a hotel in a scenic setting. When we entered it, the ballroom was filled with young Chinese couples dancing to classic western "society music" from the 1940's and 1950's, like Glen Miller's *In the Mood*. The music was upbeat and made me want to cut in for a spin around the floor. Not wanting to cause an international incident, I chickened out on that notion. But the very familiar sounds and scene evoked a pang of homesickness, despite the different faces on the dancers.

Our bus made a stop at a viewpoint to the frontier border with Red China. We couldn't see much, unlike the border points with the East Bloc countries in Europe which had several layers of barbed wire fencing and land mines in between. While looking to the 'frontier' had interest at that time because the PRC was closed to Americans, a few years later it was of low interest after Nixon made his historic trip to meet with Mao and Chou En Lai in Beijing to normalize relations.

Getting back to the 91st from Hong Kong turned out to be a bit of an unexpected adventure. I met up with a couple of our corpsmen at Tan Son Nhut airbase when returning from Hong Kong. We got on a C-130 cargo plane for our flight up-country to Da Nang. This time our plane had cargo seats, so it was more comfortable than my first flight up-country sitting on the flat, metal pallets.

That said, Da Nang was socked in with clouds and our pilot kept circling the area. Sometimes, we veered sharply. I knew that there were mountains not too far from the city and near the airfield. At this point, I had the vision that many GIs get when their time in the war zone is short or about over: would I die just short of my DEROS date? Our plane took off later for Chu Lai and our fears proved unwarranted.

NOTES:

1. When I revisited the 91st Evac site in Chu Lai in 2019, you could still make out the contours of that amphitheater in the overgrown hillside next to our site.

2. Try as I may to find any references of a sea worm/Ascaris which are edible, I could not. I did find references to a 'pig worm' which resembles a piece of the human male's anatomy which is favored by Koreans. However, that is not what was on our plate at the Indonesian restaurant.

3. Tiger Balm gardens and the mansion with it were demolished in 2004 to

make way for development. In 1971, many Hong Kong-ers regarded it as their Disneyland.

4. Tai Pak amusement park, I believe, is no longer and has been replaced with more modern parks, including a Disneyland.

Peaceful beach scene at Repulse Bay on Victoria Island.

Bamboo scaffolding surrounding new high-rise construction.

22. New Year's Eve Guard Duty

Guard duty is always a necessary but an extra duty for both enlisted men and officers. It was no different for the 91st. With our compound being at the coast edge of Chu Lai, we had three guard towers perched on the cliff overlooking the South China Sea. Our duty was to keep watch on the coast, ensuring that no one came ashore after dark. The local Vietnamese fishermen would put out in their LRBs to tend fishing seines at night. The worry was that the enemy would come ashore posing as a fisherman to blow up some target. During my year at the 91st I don't think this ever happened, at least in our patrol area.

Our nightly crew would be fourteen: three guys to man each of the towers, another three for the main gate, a senior NCO (Sergeant of the Guard, SG), and an OG (Officer of the Guard). With three guys in a tower, we planned that two could sleep while one remained on watch. The OG's and SG's job was to circulate through the towers and the front gate to check that at least one guy was always awake at each post. The crew's job at the main gate was to keep non-91st personnel out after curfew at midnight until we opened in the morning.

About a day or two in advance of New Year's Eve 1971, a junior officer from Americal HQ came to tell us that the MPs would be cracking down on the use of illumination flares to celebrate the New Year. Illumination flares are the ones that shoot up and provide light for troops to spot enemy in the dark. These flares have a parachute that slows the descent of the light, giving a good amount of time to look for enemy movement. A GI holds the flare canister in their hand with the top pointed up in the air in the direction they want it to go and hits the base abruptly on the ground to activate it to shoot up.

The officer described as "prohibitively high" the cost to replenish flares from GIs shooting them off at midnight on New Year's Eve. He warned that the MPs would be stationed around the base camp to identify any guard towers violating Command's orders. So, here's an instance where I should have remembered my Dad's advice of "Don't take any wooden nickels" and not taken the MP officer's warning to heart.

As I caught OG duty on New Year's Eve, I dutifully related to my crew that night about the consequences of setting off their flares. I reiterated this warning on my rounds checking on the towers. I am happy to report that none of the 91st Evac guards fired their flares that night. However, at midnight one or two flares from other units went up, and then, many followed, too numerous to count. The display was not unlike Boston's Fourth of July fireworks celebration where the Boston Pops plays Tchaikowsky's *1812 Overture* from the Esplanade.

Not realizing it at the time, I got a life lesson in what in business would not constitute a "best practice." That is, Command obviously misjudged rank and file's willingness to comply with their order. They might have gotten more compliance had they offered a "carrot" for every returned flare, rather than the "stick" of punishment for firing off their flares. Command hadn't considered that no MP patrol was going to be able to handle that level of violation. In my business life after my Army years, I saw too often where upper management promulgated a new policy or objective but failed to reward for compliance or achieving the goals. The bottom line: If you want to change behavior, you must measure compliance and reward for it.

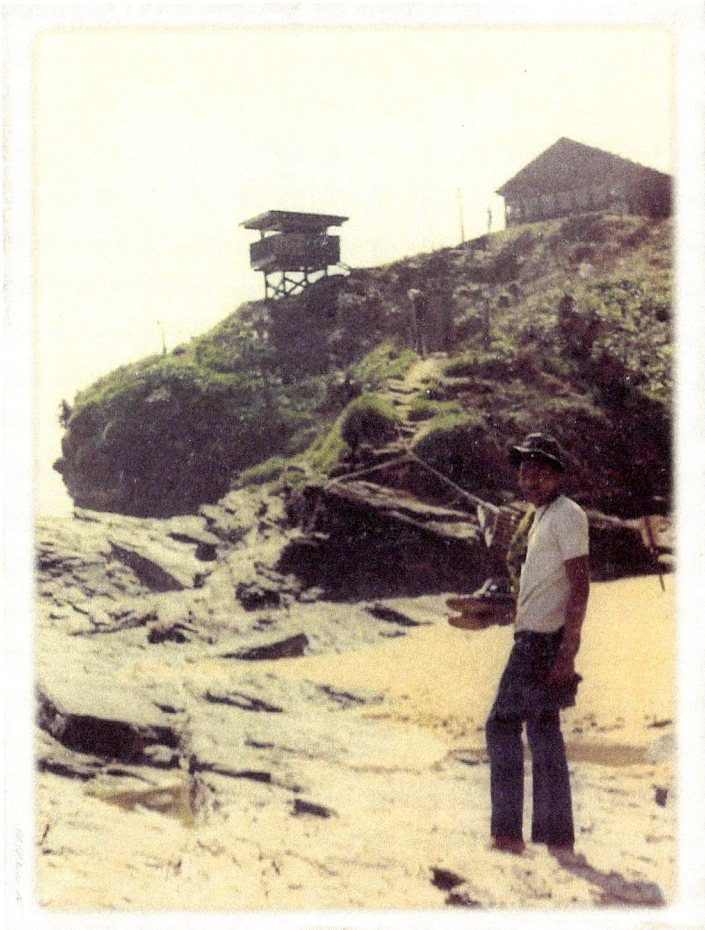

View of guard tower and O-Club from beach.

Guard tower close up. Note thick walls for sandbag protection.

23. Chief Nurses at the 91st Evac

When I arrived at the 91st, the senior nurse was a male LTC; about 50-something, graying hair with a buzzcut. He seemed to be a sociable guy who got along with the doctors and MSCs. I can't say how much the nurses liked him, or not. He possessed a positive, outgoing attitude, sort of the nursing equivalent to our XO, LTC Gipson.

In any case, he returned to the States a few months after I had arrived. His replacement was a middle-aged, female, LTC nurse who was all sinew and gristle. One might say she physically resembled a younger Irene Ryan, the actress who played Granny on the *Beverly Hillbillies*. She transferred in from another hospital in Vietnam. As a careerist, it was clear that she had high expectations of her staff and seemed to crack down on some of the laxed ways that heretofore were ignored in her predecessor's administration. She didn't suffer fools lightly.

The new chief nurse's expectation didn't play just within her bailiwick, the nurses. She stuck her nose into some of the MSC's world as well. I never had an instance of crossing paths with her on any issue with the motor pool. Maybe Warren Brennan, our

Adjutant, and Elmo Vinas, our Registrar, had more occasion to interact with her.

At some point in the spring of 1971, Warren Brennan told us that our beloved Chief Nurse was DEROSing and headed to US-AMedTC at Ft. Sam, along with a promotion to full bird colonel, COL. He wanted suggestions for a special departing gift for her. I suggested giving her a plaque from the 91st Evac's MSC to give her equal standing with USAMedTC's XO, COL "Blackjack" Jack Watson. COL Watson was similarly a no-nonsense leader who demanded white-wall haircuts, starched fatigues, and spit-polished boots of his junior officers. He got his nickname because he'd strut around the training center with a pair of black leather gloves in his hand, like some officers of his generation who carried a "swagger stick."

I remembered when I met him in his office on my first day at USAMedTC, he had a plaque on his wall from his unit in Korea. A pair of leather gloves painted gold, were mounted on the plaque above the inscription to COL Watson. I suggested that we mount a pair of gold painted, deuce-and-a-half lug nuts on a similar plaque. Our message was that this colonel, a woman, still had a pair of brass nuts/balls, and not to fool with her.

Everyone bought into the proposal. Jim Robbins, my hooch mate, volunteered to cut out the shield for the plaque from leftover plywood and he got a little brass plate engraved at the PX for it. I went to the motor pool and got two lug nuts from Woody, who welded them to two screws to allow for mounting. Voila, we had the proposed plaque in hand the night before her departure ceremony. When I showed the finished plaque to my MSC colleagues, a weak-kneed epidemic hit. Some were particularly concerned about the possible negative fallout that might come our way. Maybe in today's business climate such hesitation would be certainly justified.

The sendoff ceremony in COL Nelson's office was to take place at 2:00 or 3:00 that afternoon. I was sitting in my hooch about a half-hour before the event a little dejected after the effort we'd put into the plaque. A knock at the door came from our Sergeant Major. "Hi, Top. What's up?" I asked.

He said, "It's time to assemble for the COL's farewell ceremony. Time to go."

I acknowledged this and started out of my hooch. Then he said, "I hear you have a special present for our colonel."

I explained, "I thought I had, but my colleagues think we shouldn't give it to her."

He asked to see it and then he said, "Bullshit, you're giving it to her."

When it came time to present the plaque to her, I told her about what was on Blackjack Watson's wall, and we hoped this would give her equal standing with him in USAMedTC. Everyone held their breaths as she took it in her hands.

She loved it! She got the meaning and appreciated it. What's more our CO, COL Nelson, loved that she loved it, so much so, that he mentioned it in a letter of recommendation he gave me for my applications to medical schools after I returned to the States. Having follow through on a good collaborative idea became another life lesson that day. Too often folks have good ideas or solutions but don't act on them.

One more chief nurse I need to mention. On a lovely, sunny spring day, I passed a tall, lanky, blond, attractive, middle-aged nurse walking down the boardwalk toward the hospital orderly room. She wasn't part of our staff and she sported full-bird colonel eagles on her fatigues. She asked if she was headed in the right direction to COL Nelson's office, which I confirmed.

Later that day I was in the orderly room and asked Warren

who the visitor was that looked like Sally Kellerman in M*A*S*H? COL Nelson overheard our conversation and guffawed, "You mean that the Chief Nurse of ALL nursing in Vietnam looks like 'Hot Lips' Houlihan? She might feel it's a compliment when I tell her!" (Cue *Suicide is Painless*, the M*A*S*H theme song.)

24. Chu Lai Rocket Attacks

Rocket attacks posed the main enemy threat to the Chu Lai base camp. The rockets measured 122mm (4.8") in diameter and 75 inches long with a range of 3,000 to 11,000 meters. These were often set up with a tripod made from bamboo. In moods of black humor, we used to imagine a North Vietnamese papa-san traveling down the Ho Chi Minh trail through the jungle with one of these rockets strapped to his bicycle. We'd imagine that he'd slog it through the monsoon rains and jungle heat. Only after getting it to the mountain col near Chu Lai, the "rocket pocket," and setting it up, would he find out after lighting the fuse it was a dud[1].

I once asked Warren Brennan after I arrived at the 91st, "How do you know we're under a rocket attack?"

He replied, "You'll know; it's a bang that's distinctive."

While not the most useful of descriptions, you'd know when one hit within the greater Chu Lai area. The report/explosion was like some 4th of July fireworks designed just to deliver a big bang. I remember attending at 4th of July show two years after returning from Vietnam and when one of those big-bangers exploded, my guts puckered like it did back at the 91st.

We didn't have many rocket attacks at Chu Lai during my time at the 91st. Also, we felt that our hospital was not a primary target for the enemy rockets. However, the American Division's HQ nearby would have been. So, hits to our compound would count as "collateral damage." We probably had about five incidents in the year I was there. Maybe there were more in prior years.

The most lethal attack occurred in 1969 when a rocket hit near one of the medical wards and a piece of shrapnel entered through the Quonset hut roof and killed 1LT Sharon Lane on June 8th. The next closest rocket hitting our compound struck the cliff just below our Sergeant Major's hooch perched at the edge of the bluff. I think he and his hooch mates weren't inside at the time. Most other rockets hit an open area.

One memorable attack happened on a night when I was Officer of the Guard. My job was to check our personnel bunkers as well as the guard towers. Were our armed bunker guards alert, and the docs, nurses, and corpsmen inside protected? Making the rounds at night in a blackout added an extra level of difficulty.

The flak jackets in Vietnam were thick, heavy, and hot to wear. Many GIs wouldn't zip them up, reducing their effectiveness. I was grateful that I wasn't one of those guys this night. "Top" and I were making our rounds and were heading from the front gate guard's position into the compound toward the corpsmen's barracks and the supply buildings. Top suggested turning on his flashlight, a suggestion I nixed as a security risk, as even a lit cigarette is enough light to offer a target for a sniper. Just as I said this, Top said, "Lieutenant Boyce, where are you? You just disappeared!"

How did I do this? We had cut through my Motor Pool, and I had walked into our four-feet deep, grease pit, which had concrete walls on three sides. My right side hit the edge of one side, striking a heavy blow to my ribs. Luckily, my flak jacket padded the impact. While I was sore for the next day or two, I hadn't suffered a broken rib.

Given this low level of occurrence, many of the docs took a blasé attitude when the warning alarms went off. Protocol said they should take shelter in bunkers with their flak jackets and steel helmets. This attitude changed dramatically in February of 1971. At that time all the offensive units in Chu Lai had been deployed to support the ARVN invasion of Laos to clean out the NVA supply depots in an operation called Lam Son 719[2]. The NVA started sending multiple rockets at 8-hour intervals. It may have been the second of these attacks we heard a high-velocity roar overhead preceding another explosion. One doc who would have heretofore sauntered to a bunker at a leisurely pace, dropped to the ground outside my hooch, his helmet fell to one side, and he clamored to get his flak jacket on. His movements were reminiscent of the hapless comic GI in an old Audie Murphy or John Wayne war movie. He asked me what was going on, an answer I didn't have. While this memory is a bit humorous now, I shared the doc's concern about the screaming sounds we were hearing.

After the all-clear sirens went off, I learned that the high velocity screaming sounds came from a Navy battleship that had moved into position to protect Chu Lai. The unsettling sounds were from 8-inch munitions being fired at the enemy in the 'rocket pocket' in the mountains and those rounds were flying over Chu Lai on their way to the target. These guns were controlled by the ship's radar and computers. Radar would track the trajectory of the incoming enemy rockets and the ship's computers would back-calculate its origins and return fire. Impressive but I wish we'd been told about our protection in advance!

———

NOTES:

1. In 2019 I revisited Chu Lai and met with two NVA veterans at the 91st Evac

147

site. One had been a commander of troops in the area during the "American War." He corrected our humorous vision by saying that the 122m rockets came in three pieces and were assembled just before launching. He did confirm that there was no accurate aiming system for them. "We'd just fire them in the general direction and hope we'd hit something."

2. According to Lewis Sorley in his 1999 book *A Better War*: Harcourt, Inc.; San Diego, p.308. Lam Som 719, along with the Cambodian invasion a year and a half before, was devastating to the NVA's ability to wage war as it took a couple of years to rebuild their supplies along the border.. Had not US politicians restricted the use of carpet bombing of the Ho Chi Minh Trail through Laos and Cambodia, and the military's ability to invade North Vietnam, a different outcome might have occurred.

25. Pinch-hitting Surgeons

Between my hooch mate, Jim Robbins, and Jerry[1], a nurse anesthetist, my neighbor in the next hooch, I got into the OR to view a couple of surgeries. I've already mentioned the two laparotomies of a GI and a girl-san who had perforated guts from shrapnel. Of interest after the surgeon had finished the procedure to the point of having sutured the abdominal muscles with wire, he let the OR corpsmen finish stitching the outer layers of skin. I was impressed that they were able to do that. That said, I heard that sometimes a surgeon would have to talk his OR corpsmen through a procedure because he was unsure of his capabilities. These instances occurred when a day-shift surgeon got called out from an evening party in less than the best condition for surgery.

A craniotomy became the third surgery I got to sit in on. What an experience! A small piece of shrapnel made a small hole in a GI's scalp, about the size of a BB. First, the surgeon cut through the scalp and the connective tissue underneath, revealing the bright white bone of the skull.

Next, the surgeon asked for the Smith Cranial Perforator. What was this? The SCP resembled a 1/2" drill equipped with a ¾" bit and a stop collar that prevents the bit from penetrating any deeper than the bone thickness. He could have been in the wood-shop with the instrument throwing out chips of bone as it went into the skull. He drilled several holes, about 1" apart around the hole where the shrapnel had entered the skull. Next, he removed the bone between the holes with an instrument called ronguers, which looked like slip-joint pliers but could crunch out the bone between its jaws.

After removing the skull bone piece, he gently probed the lobes of the brain to find the source of the bleed. He found it when a huge clot floated up to the surface. He proceeded to cauterize the bleeders and once satisfied that he got them all, he closed the entry area and bandaged his head. The GI would need a later operation to put in a plate to replace the removed skull bone.

A most remarkable job change happened with our dentist, CPT Meyer Schwartz[2]. In the spring of 1971, the 91st was the busiest hospital in Vietnam. However, we were short on surgeons. So, COL Nelson, a thoracic surgeon, asked CPT Schwartz to OJT as a thoracic surgeon and Meyer accepted. Meyer took to the job change and performed surgeries in keeping with his abilities. He thought that once he returned to the States that he might seek training to professionally change his career to surgery. Logically, dental school has much of the same coursework as medical schools, and dentists typically have a high degree of small motor skills for intricate and delicate work in drilling and filling teeth. Again, we saw a situation where people pulled together to fill a need for the greater good.

NOTES:

1. I regret that I forgot Jerry's last name. He was an Army careerist and had transferred to the 91st from the Army hospital at Ft Bliss, in El Paso, TX.

Jerry made the hottest chili that I've ever tasted and taught us to eat saltines, rather than drink water to cool the heat. Also, he came with a box of tools that included power saws and drills.

2.   Again, I apologize if I have mis-remembered our dentist's name.

26. Return to the World

The standard tour of duty in Vietnam ran 12 months, although some soldiers could extend for an extra six months in exchange for being able to avoid any more active-duty service. My tour turned out to be 11 months and 23 days when I was asked to escort a heroin addict from our unit to Cam Ranh Bay a week before my DEROS date. He had to go into detox before he could return to the US. The Cam Ranh Bay out-processing center became the location of "Tricky Dick's (Nixon's) Piss Point." Once you arrived there, you went to an outdoor latrine to pee in a bottle while a staff member observed to ensure you didn't bring in a sample of "clean" urine to submit instead of your own.

My departure from the 91st came like the way the M*A*S*H movie, ended. Out of the blue one afternoon I was called to the orderly room and told by our third XO that they wanted me to escort this guy to Cam Ranh Bay. I was a week short of my DEROS date. He asked me if I wanted to go early. ("Hell, yes!" in my mind;) "Yes, Sir," from my lips.

I didn't have much time to collect my things. Jim was in our hooch, just having gotten off his shift, so I got to say good-by to him. Jim would return to the States about two weeks later.

I didn't have much time to get my guy down to the airfield; but we made it without too much time to spare. I remember wondering how the airmen acting as gate agents got through their year in Vietnam. That is, how did they feel about putting guys on planes to Cam Rahn Bay every day to go back home while they had to remain in Chu Lai until their DEROS date?

I never saw my guy after we gave our urine samples as he would have been taken to another area to start detox. He had to be clean before he could get his trip back home.

I don't remember how long I waited in the Cam Rahn Bay transfer unit before I got on my "Freedom Bird" flight back home. I do remember watching a young Martin Sheen, Patricia Neal, and Jack Albertson in a depressing movie, *The Subject Was Roses*. It was about a returning WWII vet to his home where his parents argued all the time.

I did take the time to write a note to Jim Robbins and John Rink in the motor pool about what to expect when they got to Cam Rahn Bay. I was allowed to keep one set of jungle fatigues which I still have the shirt today and have used for fly fishing.

I boarded the TIA plane in my khakis with guys from units all over. I had expected to hear a cheer as we took off, but none emerged. That said, Three Dog Night's *Joy to the World* was playing in my mind! I guess it was the fear that the enemy might down our jet with a SAM rocket that they used on our fighter jets. On the other hand, some vocal acknowledgement erupted when the flight attendant announced our landing at SeaTac airport. Buses took us from the airport to Ft Lewis for out-processing.

We had to spend about a day at Ft. Lewis, WA, which included an exit physical and signing paperwork that I had no medical issues attributed to my service in the Army. In an orientation we were told that we'd most likely not have to serve in the Army

Reserve since we'd been in Vietnam. Believing this promise eventually became another "wooden nickel" I accepted.

Jean was happy to have me home but Lee at 19 months didn't really know who this guy was that came to live with him. I remember Jean holding him after waking up from his nap on my first afternoon in our apartment in Amherst, MA. He recoiled in her arms after I gave her a kiss and went to give him one. He gave me what we now call, "the stink eye." It sunk into me how much I had missed at home in the year away.

Five days after DEROSing from Vietnam, I was sitting in a graduate level Cell Physiology class at University of Massachusetts, Amherst. This reality was hard to grasp, only second to taking my GRE test in a trailer in Chu Lai, next to a very active helipad. The last time I took a test like that was second semester, senior year at Rutgers where I was sitting in an ivy-covered building at the Princeton University testing center taking the MCAT. At UMass I stuck out in my outward appearance with my short hair and khaki slacks on a campus where long hair, beards, work shirts, and jeans prevailed.

I had been conditionally admitted as a first-year graduate student in the Department of Biochemistry. I had to do well on the Cell Physiology summer course and my first semester courses. As I had not been a Chem major at Rutgers, I had to take more courses than the other people in my first-year class. My course load that first year demanded a lot of my time, but my mind was like a sponge. The two-year break from university life became an unexpected plus of my military duty.

Long-story short, I did well enough my first year that the department admitted me as regular graduate student. I finally graduated with my Ph.D. in biochemistry and pursued a rewarding career in industry, rather than in academia.

I don't remember exactly where I had heard it. It might have been a letter I got from Jim Robbins or from my cousin, Tommy, who'd been with the 101st Airborne in Phu Bai. Typhoon Hester hit Chu Lai[2] on October 23rd, four months after I DEROSed with 115 mph winds and destroyed so many buildings that they closed the 91st Evac down, rather than rebuild.

Due to the lottery system for the draft, the demand to join reserve and National Guard units evaporated. Therefore, declining enrollment numbers led to me getting a notice that I would have to serve my remaining four years of service obligation[1] in the Army Reserve. Luckily, I was able to satisfy my remaining Army Reserve obligation in a MobDes (Mobilization Designee) program for the next five years.

As a MobDes officer in the case of a major mobilization, I'd replace an MSC officer in a Stateside unit while he deployed overseas. In my case, I'd replace the hospital clinical lab officer, an LTC MSC, at Fort Meade, MD. When I reported to him my first summer assignment, he said, "I know they assigned you to replace me in case of a national emergency, but there is no way you'll be able to do my job." How about that as a welcoming statement? Big difference to Warren's when I arrived at the 91st.

In a way he was probably right as clinical chemistry focuses on analyzing blood and urine using specific assays with known limits for normal readings. While my biochemistry studies involved similar methodologies, these didn't involve medical sample analyses. So, I invested in a Clinical Chemistry textbook to bone up on those methods. My boss's attitude seemed more accepting my second summer as he assigned me a project to evaluate a new electrophoresis method of checking blood samples for sickle cell hemoglobin versus normal hemoglobin. I only had to do my two-week duty at Ft. Meade twice in the next five years, probably due to the RIF (Reduction in Force) for the military at that time.

I'd like to say that Jean, Lee, and I lived happily ever after, but we didn't. We divorced three years later, due mainly to incompatible values, not any Vietnam War/PTSD, related issues. She went on to complete her EdD degree at UMass, Amherst, and had a successful career as a professor in business systems with the state university systems of New York and Maryland.

I met Ellen, my wife of forty-three years, a year after my divorce. We raised three children, living in New York state, Denmark, England, and North Carolina. To my utter surprise, my Vietnam experience surfaced 30 years after my tour when we were at an outdoor holiday concert at Meredith College in Raleigh. Peter, Paul & Mary were performing with the NC Symphony Orchestra on a pleasant late summer evening. When Mary Travers broke into her lead on *Leaving on a Jet Plane*, tears emerged, and I didn't know where they came from. That song always brought the feelings of homesickness to my gut when I heard it during my tour at the 91st.

NOTES:

1. 1. In my time, healthy males over 18 owed six years of military service. If you were drafted or had a ROTC commissioned in the Army Reserve, you had to do two years of active duty and four years in the Reserve. For those who "enlisted for the draft" they owed three years of active duty and three in the Reserve. Officers getting a Regular Army commission owed a minimum of four years on active duty and two in the Army Reserves, if they didn't choose to remain on active duty for a career.
2. Story in Pacific Stars and Stripes, October 25, 1971.

.

27. Chu Lai Revisited

The 2019 wedding of a friends' son to a lovely Vietnamese woman precipitated our making arrangements to travel back to Vietnam. We contracted with a travel agent specializing in Asian touring who set up visits in Hanoi, Dalat, Hoi An outside Da Nang, Hue, and Saigon. Despite my positive memories of my tour of duty in Chu Lai, I had heard from others to expect Vietnam to be different as the country has moved on from their "American War."

When our plane landed in Da Nang on our way to Hoi An, I started to realize just how much had changed. Chinese investment had grub staked much of the change, some wanted, some not. The road by China Beach in Da Nang illustrated one such quantum leap change. The one-time, two-lane road with potholes morphed into a four-lane divided boulevard lined with luxury hotels and gated resort communities. You might think you were driving in some beach resort in Florida. Hanoi, Da Nang, and Saigon/Ho Chi Minh City have many impressive glass and steel high rises that compete with what one sees in Miami and LA. These cities also have a smog problem due to the many motor scooters and cars that choke the roadways.

The Vietnamese government turned down one proposed

Chinese development project to put a hotel in the mountain pass separating Da Nang from Hue. Why? Potential military value. The French built walled towers/an old fort there from the late 1800's which remain today. Also, the US used that location for artillery to provide covering fire to the Da Nang coastal plain during the war.

On our trip we learned that the Vietnamese, Cambodians, and Thais all remain vigilant and a bit distrustful of their "Big Brother" to the north. After the end of the American War, the Chinese invaded Vietnam in the north in 1979. The Vietnamese successfully beat the Chinese back across the border.

At some point in organizing our tour, our travel agent asked, "Would you be willing to meet with some local vets when you're in Chu Lai?" I replied, "Yes," a little too quickly. After I made the commitment, I got to thinking, "What local vets? Would they be ARVN (Army Republic Viet Nam, i.e., South Viet Nam), NVA (North Vietnamese Army) or VC (Viet Cong)?" It turned out I met with a man and a woman from the NVA. He had been a local commander in the area and became Chu Lai's mayor after the war. The woman said she worked in the NVA battalion HQ during the war. In our post-trip debrief, I told our travel agent that vets who had engaged in active combat with the enemy during the war probably might not appreciate such an invitation.

As it turns out, the many telephone calls to confirm our meet up from the provincial government offices in Tam Ky began to unnerve our guide. They called about six or seven times over three days to inquire if we were still coming. Few of our different guides, if any, had occasion to escort a returning vet to their tour of duty sites, but they were all very curious.

The drive down from Hoi An to Chu Lai on the main road had changed a lot since the one time I made it with Woody, my motor sergeant. Then, open fields and rice paddies with kids walking the banks with their water buffalo following along bordered much of the 60 kilometers of Route 1 between Da Nang and Chu Lai. Now, the road is lined by buildings at the edge of the road most of the way. The day was grey, and rain threatened, as it was the northern monsoon season, just like the day Danny our corpsman died during my tour. Most of my memories are of the sunny days with cerulean blue skies, as you'll see in the photos in this book.

I knew we were getting into Tam Ky after we passed the Buddhist temple in the middle of town. I didn't see the Catholic church that used to be right next to it. Had it moved, or did the communist government have it removed? A new, modern concrete highway bridge replaced the steel trestle bridge that had been blown up and laying in the river on that trip with Woody. Progress all around.

We stopped first at a provincial office building in Tam Ky. The president of the local veteran's association first greeted us. He served in the military after 1975 after the American involvement but in time for the Chinese invasion in 1979. Afterwards, he introduced us to the two "American War" vets who appeared in their old uniforms.

Two politicos, a young man and woman, joined our party to visit the site of the 91st Evac site. Our guide wasn't sure of what their function was. Were they 'watchers" to make sure no one made any "career ending" statements? Or, just interested in seeing what an American War vet looked like?

We turned left off the main road after passing a huge THACO truck and bus assembly plant and ascended a small rise to the spit of land where the 91st stood 48 years ago. Today it's a fallow field area being overgrown with scrub bushes. Where there was grass, there were "pasture patties" meaning that someone was letting cattle graze there. On the adjacent hillside we could make out the outline of the Bob Hope Show amphitheater built in 1967. Some crumbling macadam remained underfoot at the entrance to our compound. I located our motor pool area when I came across the concrete walls of our grease pit. Today, shrubs and weeds have sprouted up from its once oil-stained earthen bottom. A couple of beaten herd paths radiated out towards the cliffs approximating the location of our compound roads, one due east past where the motor pool and supply buildings had been. One path led to the cliff, roughly where our mess hall stood. Following it, I discovered that the cliff had fallen, dumping tons of clay onto part of our old beach. One of the locals said that the young people call our old beach, "Honeymoon Beach," possibly owing to the secluded nature of its location?

When we were at the motor pool area, Ellen, my wife, asked, "How do you know this is where it is?" I pointed to the concrete remains of the grease pit and said, "This is our grease pit."

Ellen asked, "How do you know that?"

I replied, "Because I fell into it during a blackout."

Unbeknownst to me, Ellen recorded all of this on her iPhone. When our oldest daughter saw this video, she piped up, "Say, Dad, I didn't think you ever drank like that." I had to explain I hadn't been in an alcoholic blackout, but that Chu Lai had been under a rocket attack at night, so all lights were out, and it was pitch black.

From the old site we repaired to a seafood restaurant on the Main Beach where Tim Howard, our two docs, and I passed our lifeguard test. The South China Sea roiled angrily in winter monsoon fashion and the temperatures in the low 60's necessitating wearing a jacket at the covered, outdoor dining area. It became clear that lunch, complete with vodka, was probably the inducement for the NVA vets to meet. The politicos from Tam Ky wanted a photo op of me with their two vets, shaking hands and enjoying a lunch. I didn't like being used for some local propaganda, but I complied to keep the peace.

The former commander kept wanting to toast and kickback yet another shot of vodka. Luckily, the bottles were probably only a pint, and the shot glasses were small. Still the number of toasts mounted up. I recalled my colleagues from my business world talking about business lunches in Soviet Bloc countries where every guest got a bottle of vodka at their place setting. At some point, the woman vet refused to refill her shot glass so I knew I could soon do the same. At one point during these toasts, the local commander vet asked, "So, what do you think of Vietnam today?"

Happily, I still had the presence of mind to respond with, "It looks a whole lot better than when I left it," which seemed to please him. While true, I thought to myself, "But I wonder what it would look like if the US side had won?"

Alas, the hotels we had envisioned along the cove of Chu Lai never materialized. Instead, there has been substantial industrial development. A petroleum processing plant is located at the southern part of the cove where US tankers used to deliver jet fuel in the war. The air strip remains as Chu Lai Regional Airport and the THACO bus and truck assembly plant offers more employment opportunities.

Unanswered in my mind is what happened to the mama and papa-sans that worked at the 91st? I hope that our hooch maid, Mr. Biu, our motor pool guys, and the "Queen Bee" were not prosecuted by the victorious NVA after the war.

I also wonder about "Boy-Tan," who was about 12 when I last saw him. That would make him about 63 today. Outwardly, he seemed a typical, happy adolescent boy, but his story testifies to the ugliness and the messiness of any war. Boy Tan was an orphan because the VC had executed his parents. He came to live with one of the docs at the 91st after spending time living with a US Marine unit. When with the Marines, he would enter a village and play with the children there. He'd learn who were VC and who were not. At some point the Marines would come in and take out the VC. The VC offered a bounty on his head which is why he lived at the 91st. I hope that someone had adopted him or got him to the US. It's a pity that I'll never know.

My return visit reinforced my initial assessment that most of the people of Vietnam are hardworking people. Their welcoming nature to Americans tells me that our failed effort to prevent communism made a positive impression on some. Helping the US image are the relatively bad manners displayed by Chinese and Russian tour groups.

View toward Bob Hope Amphitheater from 91st compound entrance.

View of landslide to 91st / "Honeymoon" beach from Mess Hall location.

Our group visiting the 91st Evac site standing in front of motor pool grease pit.

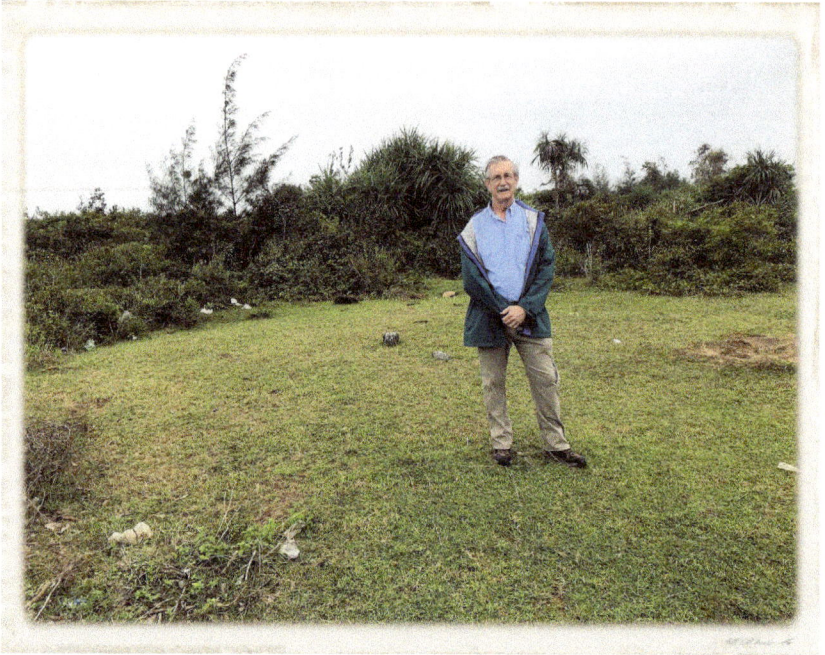

The author standing at approximate location of his hooch.

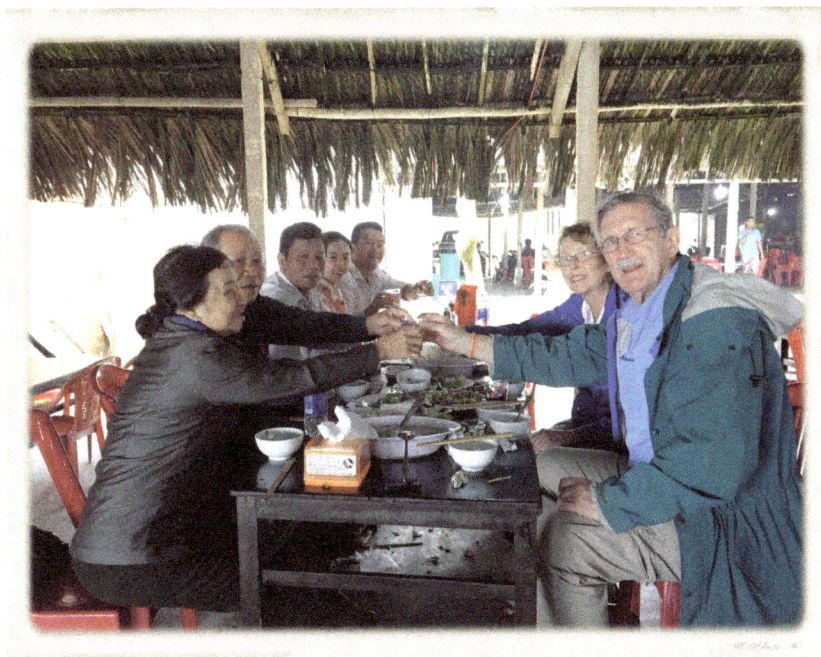

Lunch after site visit at seafood restaurant on old Main Beach.

View from Main Beach back to bluff and point where 91st Evac once stood.

28. Bao Loc Wedding

Besides my innate curiosity, another impetus for my return trip was the wedding of the son of friends of ours and a Vietnamese woman. The happy couple met and fell in love while both were working in Taiwan. They planned to be married in Bao Loc, her hometown in January 2019. We attended the wedding before our return to Chu Lai and it remains a special memory. Besides the groom's parents and an uncle, Ellen and I made up the rest of the party for the groom's side.

During the Vietnam War, the military greatly discouraged marriages between GIs and local women. A GI would have to get permission from his CO even to start the process. Permission was rarely given. I guess they were concerned about "Green Card Marriages" of convenience.

We didn't know what to expect for a Vietnamese wedding, but we were advised that karaoke would be involved at the reception party. So, I had come prepared with some lyrics for American songs. Nervous about performing in front of an audience, I had asked our guides in Hanoi and Dalat, "How big are Vietnamese weddings?" Both answered, "300 to 400 people!"

"How come so many?" I asked.

"It's an opportunity for our families to entertain/pay back their village." One of the guides whose wife came from a distant village said that he and his wife had to have a reception in each village, both with that many guests. While the young Vietnamese today might prefer a smaller, more intimate affair, their parents insist on the traditional arrangements as not doing so would mean "losing face."

Our travel agent arranged that tour guides and drivers for Dalat in the Central Highlands took care of getting us to/from Bao Loc for the wedding. (The team in Hoi An (near Da Nang) and Hue took us on the daytrip down to Chu Lai.)

The Catholic wedding with a Mass at 5:00 in the morning made for an early get up! It was the regularly scheduled early morning, weekday Mass timed to accommodate attendees who had to work in the fields. We felt a chill in the air as the sun crept over the hills around Bao Loc as we waited outside the church for the doors to open. The temps must have been in the upper 50's and we all wondered if we shouldn't have included a warmer jacket in our pack list.

As relatives and villagers gathered outside the church, I recalled the opening scenes of that Eastern Orthodox wedding in *The Deer Hunter*. Weddings bring out the same human feelings of pending excitement and a little uneasiness of the attendees you don't know. It doesn't matter whether these happen in a foreign country or a steel town in Ohio or Pennsylvania.

The Mass progressed as any other Catholic Mass except that everything was in Vietnamese. Only when we got to the exchange of vows did English creep in for the groom's benefit. The church choir sang beautifully in their claret robes and added an extra pomp to the ceremony. I wound up with an unexpected role of being an official witness to sign the marriage certificate after the

ceremony. The two official witnesses had to be non-family attendees, one each from the groom's and the bride's sides.

After the ceremony, the wedding party went back to the bride's
family home for a breakfast, a scaled back meal compared to the
rehearsal dinner the night before and the reception dinner to come.
These latter two feasts involved many splendid dishes of meats,
fish, and vegetables. Our decisions involved trying to decide how
much of any one dish to put on our plates since we had so many
choices to make. Always another delectable offering would appear
from the kitchen.

We made a cash offering as our wedding gift to the bride and
groom to help offset her parents' expense of the rehearsal dinner
and wedding reception. We also picked up a bottle of Chivas Regal
at a shop in Dalat before traveling down to Bao Loc. We learned
after our trip that if you want to be sure that you're giving authen-
tic western booze, one should buy it in a duty-free store when you
leave the US as counterfeits are prevalent elsewhere. Still, what we
brought didn't go to waste as it made the rounds to the tables with
the other bottles for toasts during the dinners.

During the reception dinner, two of the bride's aunts and a
guy from the village sang beautifully with their karaoke selections.
They certainly set a very high bar, not matched by anyone from
the groom's camp. My throat tensed a bit when I volunteered to
do a song from the groom's side. I followed the groom and his
uncle doing Steppenwolf's *Born to Be Wild*. I picked a less ambi-
tious selection, *The Gypsy Rover* by the Highwaymen. I got one of
the bride's friends to translate to Vietnamese what the song was
about, which tells of a young, roving man who won the heart of
a maiden of whom the father didn't approve. The song concludes
with learning that the young rover came from nobility elsewhere.
While I didn't totally embarrass myself, I might have done better

without the technical difficulties in coordinating the DJ's playing of the music and what I was getting on my iPhone. I'm glad to report that the happy couple now live in the Raleigh area and have started their family.

Epilogue

People often ask, "Are you sorry you went to Vietnam?" Truthfully, I am not. I felt I did it as my duty as a citizen of our country. It was a character-building experience of doing a job under stressful conditions and doing my part with others to provide a very valuable function: saving lives and healing broken bodies in a war zone. Like lacrosse, a contact sport, one must make decisions in the workaday world, take action under pressure, coordinate with teammates, all without losing one's cool. Doing so without raising your blood pressure can lead to a happier and longer life.

Personally, I believe that every able-bodied American should serve a mandatory two years of national service either after high school or college. It doesn't have to be in the armed forces but could include organizations like AmeriCorps and the Peace Corps. I have little faith in glib political leaders who haven't served but send young men and women off to a war.

Would I want to go to a warzone again? No! I have great sorrow in my heart for all those who sustained life-changing injuries or died in Vietnam, a lost cause. We've demonstrated to ourselves in Iraq and Afghanistan that the US lacks the resolve and resources to win militarily and then win the hearts and minds of the citizenry to sustain a peaceful, democratic society in the aftermath. Clearly, as documented in Lewis Sorley's book, US politicians hamstrung our armed forces in prosecuting the Vietnam War which delayed and prevented even a successful military outcome.

Despite all the sophisticated weaponry available to our armed forces today, any military victory requires "boots on the ground," men and women in the conquered territory to secure it, after all the "shock and awe." We can only hope that in any future conflict our government wants to engage in that they set the combat end goal and resolve to not interfere with the military until that goal is achieved. Certainly, we should have learned the lesson that keeping the peace after a military success is a costly proposition in terms of expense, manpower, and US public's acceptance/tolerance. Initiating any war without these terms set will constitute us accepting the "wooden nickels" of a half-baked proposition.

That said, we may be approaching such a decision with Putin's Hiter-esque war of aggression in Ukraine and China's overtures to retaking Taiwan. Let's hope that we get it right and that any future conflict does not involve nuclear weapons.

Glossary

ARVN: Army of the Republic of (South) Vietnam

BOQ: Bachelor officer quarters. Living quarters for officers without family on military posts/bases

C-130: A medium sized US Air Force cargo plane capable of taking off and landing on unimproved runways; capable of carrying 42,000 lbs of troops and/or equipment

Chu Hoi: Was a program to solicit defections from the Viet Cong. VC patients in Army hospitals in Vietnam were offered the ability to change sides. Some became scouts for Army units.

CO: Commanding officer of a unit

DEROS: Date of expected return from overseas

Duece and a Half: A medium-duty, diesel powered cargo truck capable of carrying a 5,000 lb load off-road and 10,000 load on highways.

EM: Enlisted men of all ranks

EM-Club: A gathering place for enlisted men when off-duty

Fire Base: Also termed Fire Support Base. These could be of various sizes but contained 105mm and/or 155 mm artillery pieces to provide support to infantry operations in an assigned area. These would have fortified positions, an aid station, and a tactical operations center for the infantry units.

Flak Jacket: heavy protective vests made of layers of "ballistic" nylon, weighing about 8 lbs. (Note: "ballistic" nylon refers to a type of textile weave, unrelated to ballistic projectiles.)

Frag Wounds: Puncture wounds caused by pieces of debris and/or metal fragments from an exploding device. Hand grenades had a segmented metal coil wrapped around the explosive charge. The segments would separate upon detonation spreading out to kill or incapacitate an enemy

Hooch: 16' x 32' wood-framed building with a corrugated metal roof for housing officers and senior NCOs. See photo in Chapter 8.

LBJ: Long Binh Jail, not our former president. It was designed to hold 400 prisoners but was know to hold more than 700 by 1968. Soldiers convicted in Courts Martial were sent there to serve their sentences.

LRB: Little Round Boat used by local fishermen. These were woven from reeds with tarred bottoms to keep out water. A fisherman would use a single oar to scull himself about to tend seine nets.

LZ: Landing Zone for helicopters. These could be impromptu for extricating soldiers and wounded from an area or a more permanent part of a fortified location, like a firebase.

MOS: Military Occupational Specialty. For enlisted men these were alphanumeric descriptors; e.g., 91A for medical corpsman/combat medics in Vietnam. Officers had a 4 digit descriptor for their MOS; but today, they now have an alphanumeric.

MPC: Military payment certificates. In some foreign postings, like Vietnam, soldiers were paid in MPC instead of US currency. When you return to the US, MPC would be converted back to USDs.

NCO: Non-commissioned officers empowered to lead small teams. Lowest NCO is Corporal/E-4; followed by ("buck") Sergeant/E-5/SGT. Highest ranking NCOs are Command Sergeant Majors/E-9/CSM

NVA: North Vietnam Army. A conventional, well-trainned army from the north operating in the south with supply lines running along the "Ho Chi Minh Trail" along the borders of Vietnam with Laos and Cambodia.

O-Club: Officer's club. A gathering place for commissioned officers when off-duty

OM: Operator maintenance. Those tasks the driver of a military vehicle perform, e.g., keeping tires properly inflated.

OCS: Officer Candidate School. An army training program whereby enlisted personnel can transition to commission officer.

PACEX: Pacific Exchange. Every Army post has a PX for "Post Exchange" which was a store selling goods at a reduced rate to active duty and retired Army personnel. PACEX was a larger enterprise operating out of Hong Kong but issued catalogs whereby military folks could order goods to be sent to their unit in Vietnam or to their stateside homes.

R&R: Time off from combat to rest and relax in a nice, safe area. These could be taken in-country at China Beach or Cam Rahm Bay or in out-of-country locations: Honolulu, Taipei, Sidney, Hong Kong, and Bangkok.

ROTC: Reserve Officers Training Corps. Courses and training offered on selected college campuses. It is an alternative route to become a commissioned officer in the US military.

"Top": Nickname given to any most senior NCO in a unit, usually a First Sergeant, Sergeant Major or Command Sergeant Major, depending on the size of the unit.

USO: United Service Organization. An organization dedicated to serving US military personnel and their families. In Vietnam they provided touring entertainment groups to boost the morale of our troops. Biggest of these activities was the annual Bob Hope tour.

VC: Viet Cong, "Charlie," or the local guerilla enemy. They did not wear a uniform other than black clothing. They specialized in setting boobytraps and small unit raids on patrols and firebases.

XO: Executive Officer, the second in command of a unit

About the Author

C. O. L. "Don" Boyce was born and raised in Maryland. He attended Rutgers – The State University in New Brunswick, NJ where he was commissioned as a Second Lieutenant, Medical Service Corps, upon graduation. He led training companies for Advanced Individual Training to become medical corpsmen at Ft. Sam Houston, TX. He deployed to Vietnam in July1970 and served at the 91st Evac Hospital in Chu Lai until his DEROS in

1971. Afterwards, he obtained a Ph.D. in biochemistry from the University of Massachusetts-Amherst, on the GI Bill and pursued a career in industry applying enzymes for industrial processing solutions. During his employment years he and his family resided in New York state, Denmark, England, and North Carolina. He is married and has four grown children.

Lightning Source UK Ltd.
Milton Keynes UK
UKHW021522100223
416667UK00012B/569